Data for Social Good

Jane Farmer • Anthony McCosker
Kath Albury • Amir Aryani

Data for Social Good

Non-Profit Sector Data Projects

Jane Farmer
Social Innovation Research Institute
Swinburne University of Technology
Melbourne, VIC, Australia

Kath Albury
Swinburne University of Technology
School of Social Sciences, Media, Film
& Education
Melbourne, VIC, Australia

Anthony McCosker
Social Innovation Research Institute
Swinburne University of Technology
Melbourne, VIC, Australia

Amir Aryani
Social Data Analytics Lab
Swinburne University of Technology
Melbourne, VIC, Australia

ISBN 978-981-19-5553-2   ISBN 978-981-19-5554-9 (eBook)
https://doi.org/10.1007/978-981-19-5554-9

© The Author(s) 2023. This book is an open access publication.
Open Access This book is licensed under the terms of the Creative Commons Attribution 4.0 International License (http://creativecommons.org/licenses/by/4.0/), which permits use, sharing, adaptation, distribution and reproduction in any medium or format, as long as you give appropriate credit to the original author(s) and the source, provide a link to the Creative Commons licence and indicate if changes were made.
The images or other third party material in this book are included in the book's Creative Commons licence, unless indicated otherwise in a credit line to the material. If material is not included in the book's Creative Commons licence and your intended use is not permitted by statutory regulation or exceeds the permitted use, you will need to obtain permission directly from the copyright holder.
The use of general descriptive names, registered names, trademarks, service marks, etc. in this publication does not imply, even in the absence of a specific statement, that such names are exempt from the relevant protective laws and regulations and therefore free for general use.
The publisher, the authors, and the editors are safe to assume that the advice and information in this book are believed to be true and accurate at the date of publication. Neither the publisher nor the authors or the editors give a warranty, expressed or implied, with respect to the material contained herein or for any errors or omissions that may have been made. The publisher remains neutral with regard to jurisdictional claims in published maps and institutional affiliations.

Cover illustration: Pattern © Melisa Hasan

This Palgrave Macmillan imprint is published by the registered company Springer Nature Singapore Pte Ltd.
The registered company address is: 152 Beach Road, #21-01/04 Gateway East, Singapore 189721, Singapore

Acknowledgements

We pay our respects to the traditional custodians of the lands on which we work and acknowledge their Elders, past and present.

We would like to acknowledge funders of our research on data for social good, including the Australian Research Council (ARC) for Linkage Infrastructure Equipment and Facilities, grant no. LE200100074; Data Co-operative Platform for Social Impact; the ARC Centre of Excellence for Automated Decision Making and Society, grant no. CE200100005; ARC Discovery Project, grant no. DP200100419; Victoria State Government; Australian Red Cross; Lord Mayor's Charitable Foundation; and City of Greater Bendigo Data Co-op partners.

We would like to acknowledge the contribution of the Regional Innovation Data Lab (RIDL) at Griffith University, Queensland, Australia, and the Visualisation and Decision Analytics (VIDEA) Lab at the University of Canberra, Australia.

Contents

1	**Introduction**	1
	The Non-Profit Sector and Data	4
	Making Good Use of Data	7
	Starting to Think About Data Capability	13
	Navigating Data Harms by Involving Citizens	15
	Key Takeaways from This Chapter	20
	References	21
2	**Case Studies of Data Projects**	27
	Case Study 1: Outcomes of Family Violence Policy—A Public Sector Collaboration	29
	Project Goal	29
	Project Description	29
	Collaborating Partners	31
	How the Project Began	31
	Summary of Datasets Used	32
	Methods	33
	Findings	34
	Outcomes and Lessons Learned	36

Case Study 2: Re-using Operational Data with Three Non-Profits	38
Project Goal	38
Project Description	39
Collaborating Partners	39
How the Project Began	40
Summary of Datasets Used	41
Methods	42
Data Analysis	43
Findings	44
From the Before and After Interviews	46
Outcomes and Lessons Learned	47
Case Study 3: City of Greater Bendigo Data Collaborative	48
Project Goal	48
Project Description	49
Collaborating Partners	49
How the Project Began	50
Summary of Datasets Used	51
Methods	51
Data Analysis	52
Findings	53
From the Before and After Interviews	54
Outcomes and Lessons Learned	57
Summary	58
Key Takeaways from This Chapter	60
References	61
3 Data Capability Through Collaborative Data Action	**63**
Understanding Data Capability	64
A Collaborative Data Action Methodology	67
Finding Your Data Collaborators	74
Responsible Data Governance	76
Data Ethics and Consent	79
Data Sharing for Collective Gain	83
Key Takeaways from This Chapter	84
References	85

4	**Activating for a Data-Capable Future**	89
	Sectoral Benefits of Non-profits with Data Capability	90
	Data Capability and Organisational Competence	90
	Data Capability and Field-Building	91
	Data Capability and Social Justice Activism	92
	Three Stages of Non-profits' Data Capability	93
	Data Analytics as Business as Usual	94
	Getting Started	94
	Moving Beyond a Data Project: Next Steps	98
	Innovations to Solve Data Challenges	100
	Research Reflections and Next Steps	103
	Our Research Reflections	103
	What Next in Research?	105
	Key Takeaways from This Chapter and Conclusions	107
	References	108

Appendix: The Data Innovation Ecosystem and Its Resources   113

Glossary   121

Index   125

About the Authors

Kath Albury is an Australian Research Council Future Fellow (2022–2025) in the Department of Media and Communication at Swinburne University of Technology. She is an Associate Investigator in the Australian Research Council Centre of Excellence for Automated Decision Making and Society, and a programme leader in the Social Innovation Research Institute. Kath's research investigates the intersections of digital technologies and platforms, digital literacy, data capabilities and sexual health and wellbeing. She is a co-author of *Everyday Data Cultures* (2022).

Amir Aryani leads the Social Data Analytics (SoDA) Lab at Swinburne University of Technology. The lab applies data analytics techniques for insights into health and social challenges. His expertise is in data modelling, information retrieval techniques and real-time data analysis. Amir has partnered on projects with the British Library, ORCID (US), Netherlands Data Archiving and Network Analysis (DANS) and German Institution for the Social Sciences in Germany (GESIS). His funding sources include the Australian Research Council, the Australian National Health and Medical Research Council, and the US National Institutes of Health. He has published in journals including *Nature Scientific Data* and *Frontiers in Artificial Intelligence and Applications*.

About the Authors

Jane Farmer is Director of the Social Innovation Research Institute at Swinburne University of Technology, Melbourne, Australia. Her background is as a researcher in rural health service and workforce innovation, community engagement and social enterprise. She has a keen interest in academic-practice research partnerships, innovative research methods, transdisciplinary studies and translating research into practice. Her other books include *Social Enterprise, Health and Wellbeing* (2021), *Remote and Rural Dementia Care* (2020) and *Community Co-production* (2012).

Anthony McCosker is Deputy Director of the Social Innovation Research Institute and is a Chief Investigator and Swinburne Lead for the Australian Research Council Centre of Excellence for Automated Decision Making and Society. His research addresses digital inclusion, participation and inequality and explores the impact of new communication technologies, particularly in relation to health and wellbeing and social inclusion. Current research addresses the social issues related to automation and machine vision technologies and media and the need for community-led approaches to data and analytics. He is author or co-author of numerous articles and books, including *Everyday Data Cultures* (2020), *Automating Vision: The Social Impact of the New Camera Consciousness* (2020) and *Negotiating Digital Citizenship* (2016).

List of Figures

Fig. 1.1 Taxonomy of data that non-profits might use 10
Fig. 2.1 Topic modelling analysis of Twitter topics related to family violence 2014–2018. *Note*: Ribbon graph adapted from data in "Community responses to family violence: Charting policy outcomes using novel data sources, text mining and topic modelling". by A. McCosker, J. Farmer, and A. Soltani Panah, 2020, *Swinburne University of Technology*, p. 24, https://apo.org.au/sites/default/files/resource-files/2020-03/apo-nid278041.pdf. (Copyright 2020 by Swinburne University of Technology. Adapted with permission) 36
Fig. 2.2 Timeline and peaks of Twitter activity addressing family violence by year (2015 and 2016 represented). Note: Twitter timeline analysis graph adapted from data in "Community responses to family violence: Charting policy outcomes using novel data sources, text mining and topic modelling". by A. McCosker, J. Farmer, and A. Soltani Panah, 2020, *Swinburne University of Technology*, p. 29, https://apo.org.au/sites/default/files/resource-files/2020-03/apo-nid278041.pdf. (Copyright 2020 by Swinburne University of Technology. Adapted with permission) 37
Fig. 2.3 Geospatial visualisation of three Good Cycles' employee journeys 45

Fig. 2.4　City of Greater Bendigo Community resilience dashboard layers by suburb　54
Fig. 3.1　Process of collaborative data action for non-profits' data projects　69
Fig. A.1　Initiatives and goals of the non-profits' data innovation ecosystem　114

List of Tables

Table 2.1	Summary data projects case comparison	30
Table 2.2	Data sources for public discussion of family violence	32
Table 2.3	Datasets used in the three non-profits' analyses	41
Table 2.4	Datasets for community resilience data collaborative	51
Table 3.1	Steps in the process of collaborative data action for non-profits' data projects	71
Table A.1	Tools and guides from existing initiatives	119

1

Introduction

In February 2020, just pre-COVID, a group of managers from community organisations met with us researchers about data for social good. "We want to collaborate with data," said one CEO. "We want to find the big community challenges, work together to fix them and monitor the change we make over ten years." The managers created a small, pooled fund and, through the 2020–2021 COVID lockdowns, used Zoom to workshop. Together we identified organisations' datasets, probed their strengths and weaknesses, and found ways to share and visualise data. There were early frustrations about what data was available, its 'granularity' and whether new insights about the community could be found, but about half-way through the project, there was a tipping point, and something changed. While still focused on discovery from visualisations comparing their data by suburb, the group started to talk about other benefits. Through drawing in staff from across their organisations, they saw how the work of departments could be integrated by using data, and they developed new confidence in using analytics techniques. Together, the organisations developed an understanding of each other's missions and services, while developing new relationships, trust and awareness of the possibilities of collaborating to address community needs. Managers completed the pilot having co-designed an interactive Community Resilience Dashboard, which enabled them to visualise their own organisations' data and open public data to reveal new landscapes about community financial wellbeing and social determinants of health. They agreed they also had so much more: a collective data-capable partnership, internally and across organisations, with new potential to achieve community social justice driven by data.

We use this story to signify how right now is a special—indeed critical—time for non-profit organisations and communities to build their capability to work with data. Certainly, in high-income countries, there is pressure on non-profits to operate like commercial businesses—prioritising efficiency and using data about their outputs and impacts to compete for funding. However, beyond the immediate operational horizon, non-profits can use data analytics techniques to drive community social justice and potentially impact on the institutional capability of the whole social welfare sector. Non-profits generate a lot of data but innovating with technology is not a traditional competence, and it demands infrastructure investment and specialist workforce. Given their meagre access to funding, this book examines how non-profits of different types and sizes can use data for social good and find a path to data capability. The aim is to inspire and give practical examples of how non-profits can make data useful. While there is an emerging range of novel data for social good cases around the world, the case studies featured in this book exemplify *our* research and developing thinking in experimental data projects with diverse non-profits that harnessed various types of data. We outline a way to gain data capability through collaborating internally across departments and with other external non-profits and skilled data analytics partners. We term this way of working *collaborative data action*.

By 'data for social good', we mean using contemporary data analytics techniques to fulfil a social mission or to address a social challenge. Data analytics is understood as the process of examining data to find patterns and insights that can aid decision-making and offer courses of action (Picciano, 2012). We define non-profits as all those organisations and community groups operating to pursue a social mission and that do not operate to make a profit. Individual non-profit organisations are thought of here as each pursuing their defined social mission, but also contributing to a collective social mission of achieving a more equitable and just society. While non-profits are often using data to track their operations and aid reporting, we emphasise the data that non-profits *could use* to further their work and goals. This includes mainly:

a. *internal data* generated routinely from non-profits' own operations or new data they might collect (e.g., to inform evaluation). Such data could be used, or re-used, for insights by individual non-profits or in data sharing collaboratives with other organisations and
b. *external open data* generated through government agencies or made available by other organisations.

We take a pragmatic stance here as we write at a specific point in time and from our home country context (Australia), which we acknowledge is a high-income country with neoliberal ideology influencing social policy. Non-profit data analytics is a fast-moving field where practices and legislation will change. Other countries and regions have their own nuances. Globally, the non-profit sector is on a journey with data collection and computational data analytics. This is influenced by policy that drives competition and demand for accountability and measurement, as well as a desire to use sophisticated techniques for social good. This journey will continue into the future.

This moment feels like a critical juncture for non-profits and data analytics. Current strategies and decisions taken within the sector will significantly influence both the nature of non-profit data analytics and the philosophy underpinning it, but perhaps most crucially, it will influence who has the capability to work with data and to what ends—towards what understanding of social benefit. We believe that non-profits need to have data capability to shape the future of the sector and affect the difference non-profits can make in the world. The sector can be knowledgeable, confident and advocate for suitable data practices, or—lacking capability—be forced to passively accept data practices determined by other powerful actors like government and 'Big Tech'.

This book is meant for non-profit leaders, managers, practitioners and board members who want to see what can be done with data and discover how organisations like theirs can become capable with data. It is also for researchers, as we show how partnering with non-profits can help us to contribute to social justice and to knowledge about data for social good. The book is deliberately targeted at the practice and researcher nexus.

This first chapter sets the scene by introducing concepts, challenges and our rationale for why non-profits should engage with data analytics. It is by no means comprehensive in its understanding of international data initiatives in the non-profit sector, especially not in relation to data law and guidance in different country contexts. For that, we recommend seeking out local expertise, as that area is subject to variation by country or region, and subject to change as practice is only forming.

The Non-Profit Sector and Data

The non-profit sector comprises organisations with different legal and operational structures, including charities, philanthropic foundations, voluntary and community organisations, community groups, social enterprises and co-operatives (Salamon & Sokolowski, 2018). Some non-profits generate profit but re-invest it for social purpose. The sector has different names internationally, including the charitable and non-profit sector (Canada); third sector, social economy, voluntary sector (UK); third and social economy (Europe); not-for-profit sector, community sector (Australia and New Zealand); and charitable, voluntary and philanthropic organisations, civil society (US) (Lalande, 2018; Productivity Commission, 2010; Salamon & Sokolowski, 2018). Non-governmental organisations (NGOs) are non-profits that tend to work in other country contexts (Vaughan & Arsneault, 2013).

While non-profits generally operate to address social purposes not suitably addressed by government or private organisations (Vaughan & Arsneault, 2013), the social welfare role of non-profits can vary even within countries. Indigenous cultures including the Maori of Aotearoa (New Zealand), for example, have different understandings of social and community life that influence what is considered acceptable work for community organisations. Western notions of volunteering, separation of family and community, and who should provide community services should not be regarded as automatically aligned with Indigenous Peoples' cultural understandings (Tennant et al., 2006).

In high-income countries, non-profits are significant providers of community services, including health, mental health, social care, education, environmental protection and disaster relief programmes. They contribute significantly to national economies; for example, employing around 13% of Europe's workforce (Salamon & Sokolowski, 2018). Charities alone employ one in ten workers in Australia (Social Ventures Australia and Centre for Social Impact, 2021). Beyond service provision, non-profits contribute to generating a sense of community, "giving expression to a host of interests and values—whether religious, ethnic, social, cultural, racial, professional or gender-related" (Salamon & Sokolowski, 2018, p. 56) and, importantly, act as social policy advocates (Salamon, 2014). As such, non-profits are key actors in the policy community. They influence what are recognised as societal challenges, provide evidence about fruitful solutions and influence how the work of their sector is done (Vaughan & Arsneault, 2013). Government is a major funder for non-profits in high-income countries via contracts to provide welfare services (Salamon & Sokolowski, 2018). This increasingly leads to governments dictating the terms of engagement. Consequently, it is imperative that the non-profit sector is capable in contemporary organisational practices and innovations so it can influence social policy through data-supported knowledge and ideas.

In countries where policy is imbued with neoliberal ideology, including the UK, Australia and New Zealand, increased provision of public welfare services by non-profits started in the 1980s–1990s (Tennant et al., 2006). During this time, many traditional voluntary organisations became non-profit businesses. Additionally, the trend of non-profits supplying welfare services accelerated following the 2008 Global Financial Crisis. The marketisation of the non-profit sector led to competition for funding between organisations, forcing increasing corporatisation. Some now refer to a *not-for-profit industrial complex* (*Incite! Women of Color Against Violence,* 2017), with concerns non-profits are forced to subordinate their social mission to respond to funder-determined priorities in order to survive.

Accountability and reporting demands of government and philanthropic funders mean non-profits have had to collect increasing quantities of data. Funders influence or define the data to be collected and may even supply data collection systems. This scenario can stifle non-profits' internal strategies about working with data and funnel their work towards reporting rather than using data to drive social change. To date, the sector is accused of over-emphasising easy-to-collect output data (e.g., about number of services delivered) rather than data about outcomes, impacts and the processes underpinning them (Lalande & Cave, 2017). Over time, as non-profits look for new ways to gain competitive advantage, interest in innovative data use has grown. Some larger non-profits invest in data professionals, while others contract with specialist consultants.

The danger with outsourcing data-related work is that organisational data and analytics become viewed as 'too hard' and internal know-how diminishes. We propose non-profits need to have data capability so they can appropriately drive their organisations' data strategy for impact. More widely, collectively developing data capability at a sector level enables non-profits to influence government and funder priorities and investments around social challenges *and* data practices, informed by grassroots experiences. Here, we understand *non-profit data capability* as a holistic concept that involves interconnected combinations of resources. Data capability is hard to pin down to a checklist or benchmarking tool. It involves having the staff skills and roles, technologies, data management practices and processes that are appropriate for each non-profit in relation to its context of practice and enables effective use of data within that context. Thus, data capability for a non-profit is likely to evolve, potentially in response to changing organisation priorities, learning from trying out techniques and datasets, and in response to emergent data practices and norms of the non-profit field. Non-profit data capability has foundations in responsible data governance. We suggest it can be built through collaborating, experimenting and discovering with data. We extend our discussion about non-profit data capability and how to achieve it in Chap. 3.

Unfortunately, as related to business operations rather than direct service provision, data and information management tends to be underfunded in non-profits (Social Ventures Australia and Centre for Social Impact, 2021; Tripp et al., 2020). Ongoing lack of investment and expertise in social data analytics leads to problems with adopting innovation, resulting in a phenomenon termed the *non-profit starvation cycle* (Gregory

& Howard, 2009). This is where ongoing focus on funding service delivery leaves organisations simultaneously under-invested in management and infrastructure, but also in staff skilled to understand what is required. Organisations are thus vulnerable to environmental shocks, as seen in reactions to the recent COVID-19 pandemic. A survey of Australian charities' capability to deal with the pandemic found only 46% used cloud-based systems and only a third had systems and software for working at home. Deficits were mainly attributed to underfunding (Social Ventures Australia and Centre for Social Impact, 2021). A survey and report by Australian technology non-profit Infoxchange shows that the sector has not yet prepared for advanced data analytics or for automated futures, although investment in information technology and digital infrastructure and systems is improving and the skilled workforce is expanding (Infoxchange, 2020).

Collaboration between non-profits would enable cost-sharing for infrastructure and skilled workforce, but competition in the sector is a barrier. This has led to suggestions that government should incentivise or facilitate collective working (Social Ventures Australia and Centre for Social Impact, 2021). Some successful collaborative models exist; for example, Collective Impact initiatives, where community organisations work together to identify, address and monitor change about a social challenge. LeChasseur (2016), for example, describes a *Collective Impact* initiative to improve lives of low-income mothers and their babies. In Collective Impact, collaborating with data facilitates measurement of community-level social change as well as helping to assess the contribution of individual organisations. Some non-profits are involved in initiatives funded by Social Impact Bonds, where private investment can be gained to fund projects to improve social outcomes, with outcome data required in order to access premiums (Arena et al., 2016; Sainty, 2019).

Making Good Use of Data

The main goal of non-profits using data analytics is to inform organisational learning so adaptations can be made to achieve better outcomes. A range of reasons for applying analytics techniques to data to advance social missions are outlined by Verhulst and Young (2017), including for situational awareness and impact evaluation. Once attracted by the prospect of generating such analyses, the issue for non-profits might turn to how to adapt existing datasets, departments and staff into a system capable of generating insights from data.

Data analytics for non-profits is not solely predicated on having access to technology and applying computational techniques. Rather, it builds on having a foundation of knowledge about using data in research and evaluation. In this way, as *the science of examining data*, data analytics involves considering the characteristics of data you have or can access; its provenance and how it was collected; its availability for different uses and who can access it in unprocessed or analysed versions; understanding the ethical concerns, the consent given and obtained when data was created; the quality and what is missing in the data; and who data refers to or was collected from, to understand any in-built biases and data's inclusivity. However, as well as drawing on traditional research and evaluation knowledge, data analytics also requires evolving thinking and skills as new forms of data and analytical techniques become available and new ethical principles and practices are developed in response (O'Neil & Schutt, 2013). Ultimately, *good* use of data includes careful attention to how it is generated, the widening range of data types that can be analysed, and the impact this may have on people's privacy and other rights (see Chap. 3).

Exemplifying how using new types of data requires 'old' and 'new' thinking, we used a dataset of anonymised discussions on a national online peer support forum to evaluate services for rural mental health (Farmer et al., 2020; Kamstra et al., in press). Analysis was applied to identify themes in a large qualitative dataset of posts. Moving beyond traditional approaches to service evaluation, using the forum discussions as a rich qualitative dataset meant first agreeing on a rationale for the analysis conducted, and recognising the complexities inherent in the dataset as a sample. For instance, we had to address the potential for bias given that some people were over-represented in the data (i.e., posting far more often than others). With the focus on more isolated rural service users, we removed posts made by people living in large rural towns with hospitals to ensure only more isolated residents' experiences were included. The data allowed us to access the geospatial locations of those using the online service, but when mapping quantities and themes of posts geospatially, we had to consider how to visualise the data at sufficient spatial scale and abstraction to remove any potential for identification. Thus, while computational techniques now allow analysis of much larger datasets, and new sources extend potential for social value extraction from data, many of the same basic research skills are required to intelligently conduct and interpret data analyses. Making good use of data involves navigating new possibilities, while translating traditional research skills to respond to new challenges.

Before progressing further, we now summarise the main types of external data sources and types of internal data content that we think non-profits might work with. Figure 1.1 illustrates characteristics of data we have used in our projects. It is not intended to be comprehensive of all data sources and content that could be used (for additional ideas, consult other relevant taxonomies, e.g., Susha et al., 2017).

We divide the data that non-profits might use into two categories: *internal data content* (i.e., this indicates the broad types of dataset content generated by non-profits through their work) and *external data sources* where data with a range of characteristics may be accessed. In Fig. 1.1, we suggest non-profits' internal data content can be divided into two types: *operational data*, where data is generated for and through an existing business purpose, including data about staffing, clients, services and funds; and what we term *outcome data*, referring to data collected specifically for assessing processes, outcomes or impacts of programmes. For the outcome data, what to collect is likely to be informed by a theory of change or programme logic showing links between non-profits' programmes, how they are delivered, what they achieve and the ultimate fulfilment of social mission. Typically, outcomes data might be collected through surveys at intervals following provision of programmes. *External data sources* include all data that can be accessed external to the organisation and used, including open data generated by government statistical agencies and data made into open data by other organisations. An example we have used is the *Infoxchange AskIzzy Open Data Platform* (https://opendara.askizzy.org.au/), which provides anonymised geospatial location-based data from searches for community services across Australia.

Fig. 1.1 Taxonomy of data that non-profits might use

External data also includes government and other organisations' data that can be made available under certain conditions and for particular purposes. Such data may be accessible subject to risk assessment or research protocol (e.g., sensitive government-collected health or crime data). Our understanding of 'other organisations' data extends to data from *other* non-profits, private sector organisations, academia and community groups. External data could include internal (private) datasets where data is only available to be shared within a limited collaborative group. This data will be available to the group under specific conditions through data sharing agreements as part of data sharing initiatives.

Data may be *quantitative*, for example, amount of time spent with clients, numbers of episodes of types of services delivered, distances travelled to deliver services and financial information; or *qualitative*, for example, discursive content of notes relating to clients, complaints and feedback, online forum post data. To be meaningful and relevant, analysis should also harness data that is *temporal*, for example, data capturing client needs and transactions on a daily or weekly basis over time and other forms of monitoring to enable longitudinal and even 'real time' analysis; and data that is *locational*, for example, giving a geospatial location of where services were provided or locations of clients and staff (Loukissas, 2019).

Having summarised types of data that a non-profit might use, a further issue is how they might think about sources of internal data for use in analytics. Through our work, we observe two approaches to sourcing internal data that we term here the *new data* and *re-use data* perspectives. The *new data perspective* tends to align with growth of the outcomes measurement movement (Lalande & Cave, 2017; Social Ventures Australia, 2021), where non-profits want to substantiate their social impact. This is generally handled by collecting *new data* about outcomes, impacts and processes. Where organisations initially tended to generate data through bespoke programme evaluations, more recently there is a trend to collect generic outcomes data using frameworks and data models. Using standard tools means non-profits can save effort in generating their own indicators and measures, plus a standard framework allows comparison and benchmarking across different organisations. Theoretically, funders will be able to discover which non-profits most successfully address a social challenge such as social inclusion, employment or crime prevention. Examples of these are generated by governments (e.g., the New South Wales Government Human Services Outcomes Framework, see https://www.facs.nsw.gov.au/resources/human-services-outcomes-framework) and businesses or social enterprises (e.g., Australian Social Values Bank). Researchers have also developed frameworks, for example, the *Community Services Outcomes Tree* (Wilson et al., 2021) was designed to provide "a comprehensive outcomes framework to assist services to name and then measure their outcomes…[and]… a set of data collection questions so services can ask questions of service users and collect data" (p. 1).

While such frameworks might assist cash-strapped non-profits, they have potential downsides. They imply collecting yet more data and are potentially inflexible to the nuanced interests and missions of individual non-profits. Adhering to them could drive isomorphism where programmes tend to become increasingly alike as driven by addressing a standard set of performance measures. This could hinder innovation and lead to neglecting nuanced needs of different clients and consumers. Piff (2021) highlights that non-profits could waste valuable time trying to find the perfect framework and re-orienting their data collection to meet its new requirements.

Advocacy for the *data re-use perspective* comes from policy institutes, researchers and others that are interested in combining digital social innovation with growing community and civil society data capability (Dawson McGuinness & Schank, 2021). Analysing re-used data is something of a frontier space where data scientists may partner with social scientists, lawyers, community practitioners and citizens to formulate practices that are ethical and obtain added social value from data already collected (Williams, 2020). New rules, standards, models and tools are often emergent from practical data analytics 'discovery' projects and collaborations (van Zoonen, 2020). An example of generating novel transferable tools comes from our projects with non-profits (see Chap. 2) where data protocols and data-sharing agreements were formulated through iterative discussions with data scientists, practitioners at non-profits and lawyers, where necessary.

Ultimately, of course, data must have been collected in order for it to be re-used and so the new data perspective also could generate data with potential for added value from re-use. Sometimes there may be a need for new data, but given a lot of data is already collected and exists, we advocate for optimising data re-use (where ethical and feasible) and minimising collection of new data.

As mentioned above, non-profits might work with others (non-profits and other entities) and share or pool data for richer insights and to drive collective working. Sharing data in multi-organisation collaborations is notoriously challenging (Verhulst, 2021). Understanding the extent to which data can be re-used and for what purposes, including sharing across collaborations, involves knowing why and how data was collected originally—and crucially—the details of consent obtained from those contributing to data generation (Verhulst, 2021). In the case of non-profits with their propensity to collect personal data, it often involves knowing about the nature of consent from clients, citizens and staff. Issues around consent for re-using and sharing data are explored in Chap. 3.

Starting to Think About Data Capability

Moving non-profit data analytics out of an environment of research projects and experimental initiatives and into business as usual requires comfort with using data and understanding the roles of data across the organisation and beyond. As noted above, data capability can be understood as a holistic concept, and we explore this in more detail in Chap. 3. Building data capability is not just about buying software or employing data professionals. Rather, it involves deepening knowledge and expertise in connecting the goals and work of a non-profit—their mission—with resources enabling appropriate *use of data* to meet the goals. This includes proficiency about what, where, why and how data is significant and why and how to use different data analysis techniques (Tripp et al., 2020).

It takes effort and commitment to grow organisational data capability, and there is a temptation to turn to commercial platforms and tools, like Amazon Web Services or Microsoft Azure, for data management and analysis. The challenge with implementing such tools without an organisation having done the groundwork to gain data capability is that they apply advanced analysis techniques without transparency. An organisation that invests internal know-how into identifying and implementing tools and practices that match its needs will understand potential for bias and other data harms. While we do not explore use of artificial intelligence (AI) in this book, it is coming and indeed already present in some non-profit operations and social service work. Non-profits that build their data capability will be resourced with knowledge to understand this application of data and to advocate and advise on ethical and wise use of advanced techniques.

In the context of non-profits' data work, we favour using the term *data capability*. *Data literacy* and *data maturity* are other terms applied to try to capture the idea of being 'ready' for using data. The need for citizen 'big data literacy' is widely discussed (e.g., Grzymek & Puntschuh, 2019; Müller-Peters, 2020) in the context of 'data citizenship' (Carmi et al., 2020) as a response to expanded datafication and algorithmic decision making. Sander (2020), for example, suggests this "goes beyond the skills of… changing one's social media settings, and rather constitutes …[being]… able to critically reflect upon big data collection practices, data uses and the possible risks and implications that come with these practices, as well as being capable of implementing this knowledge for a more empowered internet usage" (p. 2). One problem with using the term 'data literacy' in the context of non-profits is that it tends to target the competencies and critical awareness of *individuals* (D'Ignazio & Bhargava, 2015; Frank et al., 2016) and thus seems less suited to considering organisation-level attributes.

Similarly, we are not enthusiastic about the term 'data maturity', even though it suggests organisation-level qualities, because it conjures up the notion of an ultimate 'finish line' and doesn't account for the wide variety of circumstances that shape the use of data. We opt to talk about data capability because what we envisage are plural and dynamic qualities, situated historically and culturally, that are fundamental to fostering change across new socio-technological milieux. While ideas of data literacy and maturity help by compiling skill and competency needs, our approach is to democratise data practices, open up data expertise to all parts of an organisation and push it beyond the IT department or the bounds of appointing specialist data professionals. Our holistic conceptualisation of data capability resonates with Williams' (2020) depiction of 'data action' for public good—which is described as "a methodology, a call to action that asks us to rethink our methods of using data to improve or change policy" (p. xiii). Aligned with this call-to-action approach is a widening of data accountability, responsibility and ethics. In short, data capability involves more than ticking off attributes from a list but is about evolving understanding, resourcing, implementing and doing, involving people across organisations and in relevant communities, and interacting with changing contexts and missions.

In this book, we provide examples of how non-profits can use data and give practical strategies for non-profits to build data capability. The central approach we offer for building new capability is *collaborative data action*. Rather than consigning data solutions to individual projects or teams, we encourage collaborative processes within and across organisations. In Chap. 2, we give case studies of using collaborative data action with non-profits to generate new insights from using and re-using data. In Chap. 3, we delineate the collaborative data action methodology and highlight why it is particularly useful for non-profits. Based on our research with non-profits, we distil out key issues for non-profits to prioritise. Our mission is to put data analytics within the reach of all non-profits and to overcome isolationist and competitive data practices that concentrate capability with the well-resourced (large) few. That is, not replicating the logic of private enterprise, commercialism in data use and start-up culture exceptionalism.

Part of the 'magic' of collaborative data action is bringing together different knowledges, skills and experiences because data analytics for non-profits is a hybrid activity (Verhulst, 2021; Williams, 2020). It requires the skills of data scientists, but they tend to lack social science training. It requires social scientists with grounding in evidence and methods of social fields, and it needs practitioners because they know the practices and operating contexts of non-profit work. As non-profits' capability is built, their data work increasingly must incorporate the voice and perspectives of clients, citizens and communities. To achieve this, it is necessary to navigate the problematic environment that has arisen due to some of the ways that social data analytics has been applied to date—that is, to address the (ab)use of data causing *social harm*.

Navigating Data Harms by Involving Citizens

Part of the rationale for growing non-profits' data capability is to bridge the gap between desire to extract optimal social value from data, while addressing the risks from (re-)using this data. Much of the data non-profits generate and work with is likely to be personal data about clients and customers, perhaps sensitive and health-related data. Accountability to clients, customers and communities around use and re-use of data is paramount and challenging to execute well. At this point, as good data safety practices and technology are available, challenges are mainly due to a lack of established, evaluated models of good practice of how to work with people to formulate governance principles and processes for re-using data about them. And, building on this, how to engage citizens as empowered partners in data projects that engage with their data.

Constructing sound practices for using and re-using citizen data requires citizens at the table. In our experience of data projects with non-profits, they find it challenging even to think about holding discussions with clients and consumers about how to develop such practices. They appear afraid to mention 'the d word'. This fear of engaging with clients and consumers regarding data is linked largely to perceptions of risk due to high-profile accounts of social data *misuse*. Critical accounts of datafication emphasise the way data has become a social and political issue "not only because it concerns anyone who is connected to the Internet but also because it reconfigures relationships between states, subjects, and citizens" (Bigo et al., 2019, p. 3). Accounts about the impact of datafication on society are multiple and sometimes depict grave consequences. They exemplify harms from use of data analytics in replicating and driving inequalities of race and ethnicity, gender and class, and concentrating power in the globally dominant technology corporations (e.g., Criado-Perez, 2019; Eubanks, 2018; Noble, 2018; O'Neil, 2016; Srnicek, 2016). High-profile failures to use data and technology in social welfare settings, for example in Australia, the notorious failed Federal Government 'Robodebt' automated debt recovery programme based on welfare services data (Henriques-Gomes, 2020), are mirrored internationally. Such cases have eroded public confidence in institutions that would traditionally be trusted to care for and about citizens and data.

Different countries and regions are beginning to clarify data rights and heighten the accountable, responsible production and use of personal and social data through high-level legislation, such as the European Union's General Data Protection Regulation (GDPR) (European Parliament and the Council of the European Union, 2016), and proposed Bills to regulate Artificial Intelligence (AI). However, there is still ongoing uncertainty about what rules pertain in different contexts—and even how to find out. Data security and privacy law and responsible data governance are core elements of the context of non-profit data analytics, but we also note that risk aversion around working with data can be the immediate, and apparently easiest, response. Among non-profits highly sensitive to social injustice, vulnerabilities and systemic inequality, the idea of doing more with client and citizen data can be met with considerable anxiety, resulting in waiting until things get clearer (i.e., not re-using data). We suggest a key reason why non-profits should grow their data capability is so they can confidently and competently engage with clients, citizens and communities around responsible data use. While there are risks, and a need to proceed with caution, using citizen data for insights could bring benefits to clients, customers and the wider community. Data is already generated, so it is responsible re-use that is the central issue to be resolved. There are, arguably, three key issues to be considered in non-profits working with citizens and data: (1) developing sound data governance practices, (2) working with citizens to gain insights from data and (3) raising citizen data literacy and community data capability.

Some researchers have begun to explore how to involve 'lay' participants in discussions around responsible use of data. For example, the Data Justice Lab (Warne et al., 2021) produced a civic participation guidebook outlining participatory methods including citizens' juries and mini-publics (deliberative conversations) to discuss data use. Living labs and hackathons are other methods discussed (e.g., Flowing Data, 2013). These methods, though, tend to engage citizens in discussing large administrative or government datasets, rather than making direct links between citizens and re-use of data about them. There are some cases of active engagement of citizens with deciding about uses of their own data; for example, the Salus health data co-op in Barcelona involves people making decisions about selective use of their data (e.g., for health research), as opposed to making it entirely open or private and unavailable for re-use (Calzada, 2021). Open Humans (https://www.openhumans.org) is a non-profit dedicated to supporting individuals and communities to explore use of their data for social purposes. We found a few examples of engaging more marginalised groups about their data, and these are the citizens with which non-profits are most likely to work.

Here, perhaps, work on *Indigenous data sovereignty* indicates a useful way ahead (Kukutai & Taylor, 2016). Data sovereignty is a way of understanding the importance of establishing consent and respecting the rights of, and ensuring benefits for, those who are the subjects of data (Carroll et al., 2020). In many parts of the world, Indigenous data sovereignty working groups and scholars are defining and addressing data inequalities and exploitation among those who have had least control and benefit over data collected about them. Carroll et al. (2020) discuss the process and rationale for developing the *CARE Principles for Indigenous Data Governance*. CARE stands for: Collective benefit, Authority to control, Responsibility, Ethics; and the principles are intended as a guide for stewardship and processes to enable self-determining citizens to make decisions relating to collection, storage, analysis, use and re-use of data. The CARE principles were developed by Indigenous people due to widespread abuse of data about them involving issues of over-surveillance, use of data for policing, lack of transparency and control, and under-counting (thus under-representation). Data is as important to the sovereignty of a people as language, artefacts, landmarks, beliefs and cultural knowledge, and natural resources. As Tahu Kukutai and John Taylor eloquently argue: "missing from those conversations have been the inherent and inalienable rights and interests of indigenous peoples relating to the collection, ownership and application of data about their people, lifeways and territories" (Kukutai & Taylor, 2016, p. 2). Indigenous ways of knowing can offer new models for data governance that are built on collaborative, rather than individual or proprietary responsibility, and more respectful forms of consent. Work on Indigenous data sovereignty can offer principles for wider application to engage with citizens represented in data and who have experienced power inequities.

Moving beyond citizen engagement in designing data governance, clients and consumers should be engaged where non-profits re-use data about them. This could involve data analyses relating to, for example, situational awareness, impact assessment or for community insights. This goes beyond acknowledging people's representation in the data, but also acknowledges their vital 'lived experience' roles in ground-truthing and interpreting 'what is going on' in data analyses. Most contemporary non-profits have established relationships and ways of engaging lived-experience clients and customers in informing and enabling services so engagement with data analytics would represent an extension of such work. Partnering with citizens about data is important for informing the work of non-profits, and, as such, should be appropriately recompensed. This acknowledges the expertise of citizen clients and customers as key stakeholders in use, visualisation and interpretation of data *that is about them*. As Williams (2020) notes, involving citizens is integral because "data are people" (p. 220).

Some excellent examples of resources for involving citizens with lived experience in data projects have been generated in recent years through work of Elsa Falkenburger, Kathryn Pettit and others at the Urban Institute and specifically its National Neighborhood Indicators Partnership (NNIP; https://www.neighborhoodindicators.org/). These community data advocates devised a 'data walk' methodology to engage citizens with analysed and visualised datasets to help make decisions about their communities (Murray et al., 2015). More recently, a short *Guide to Data Chats* resource has been produced for practitioners, giving really practical advice and tools for involving citizens with data (Cohen et al., 2022). As part of the NNIP's projects, citizens are often trained to collect new, granular 'citizen science' data about aspects of living in the locale.

The NNIP sees building community data capability as a key outcome of engaging citizens in data projects. In their role as engaged with clients and customers, non-profits could be significant in developing citizen and community understanding around ethical data collection and use. As digital inclusion becomes central to social equity agendas, non-profits' data work with clients, customers and citizens could move beyond service delivery and contribute to a wider social mission of building client data literacy. This could be done by engaging people with their data, discussing issues such as sovereignty and potential to re-use data and generating co-designed data governance. Such activities would centre clients and consumers in non-profits' data practices and contribute to building data capability at community level.

Initiatives around the world are working to provide examples of ways to engage citizens, for example Our Data Bodies (https://odbproject.org) is a project working with low-income people in the US and data rights, and Amnesty International is engaging with data volunteers to help organise crowd-sourced datasets (Acton, 2020). However, specifically considering the range of large and small non-profit organisations, our experience of current practice is that non-profits' engagement of consumers and clients in re-use of their data does seem to present quite a leap. Most non-profits we have worked with are still at the stage of building their own internal data capability. As Sander (2020) concludes—with regard to citizen engagement—there is, as yet, "too little knowledge on what kind of literacy efforts work best and a lack of constructive or comprehensive research on how to address people's lack of knowledge" (p. 1). We argue that non-profits' management, boards and staff require their own data knowledge, awareness and experience as a precursor to engaging clients appropriately in conversations about data and involvement in codesign of data use practices. This is not ideal but realistic based on our experiences. Until this time, it is imperative that non-profits understand the consent they have to gather, using this knowledge to work within general ethical parameters (Williams, 2020).

Key Takeaways from This Chapter

In this chapter, we set the scene and introduce some key ideas about why and how non-profits need to engage with data analytics. The key points we'd like readers to take away are listed below.

> **Key Takeaways**
>
> - Non-profits should have the same access to data capability as commercial businesses. They should build data capability so they can inform data strategy for their organisation and the sector.
> - Non-profits should resist generating new data if possible, rather they should explore ways to re-use data they already generate and use open social data instead.
> - Once non-profits build their organisational data capability, they are well-placed to work with clients and citizens to help build wider digital inclusion and community data capability.
> - Non-profit data analytics is a hybrid space that, at its best, draws on multiple areas of knowledge, expertise and lived experience.

In the next chapter, we present case studies that illustrate our journey of working with non-profits and data, from an earlier example of working largely with social media data and government consultation submissions, to working with non-profits exploring their own data, to generating a data collaborative with non-profits and other organisations taking a place-based approach (Chap. 2). We present our case studies in Chap. 2, to give a picture of the different kinds of data projects we are talking about in this book, but also because it was working on these projects that led to the understanding of data capability we suggest here and our appreciation of the benefits of working collaboratively. In Chap. 3, we build out from those learnings from the case studies. We more fully describe what data capability for non-profits looks like and outline the collaborative data action methodology that we generated and refined while working on the case study projects and reflecting on similar work elsewhere. In Chap. 4, we look to the future—discussing the way ahead for non-profits and data analytics for social good and suggesting research and practice priorities. Data practices and regulation are dynamic and rapidly changing so there will be new work that constantly refreshes and extends what we say here. Our focus in this book is on what we gleaned from very practical projects with practitioner partners. We note the book does not provide a comprehensive international scoping of all uses of data for social good or initiatives. Rather, here we tend to highlight the initiatives and resources that we have drawn on most in developing our work (see appendix for specific detail of these). We hope this book gives help and inspiration to non-profits seeking data analytics for social good and researchers working alongside them.

References

Acton, D. (2020). *Designing Amnesty Decoders: How we design data-driven research projects*. Amnesty International: Citizen Evidence Lab. Retrieved July 15, 2022, from https://citizenevidence.org/2020/10/09/designing-amnesty-decoders-how-we-design-data-driven-research-projects/

Arena, M., Bengo, I., Calderini, M., & Chiodo, V. (2016). Social impact bonds: Blockbuster or flash in a pan? *International Journal of Public Administration, 39*(12), 927–939. https://doi.org/10.1080/01900692.2015.1057852

Bigo, D., Isin, E., & Ruppert, E. (Eds.). (2019). *Data politics: Worlds, subjects, rights.* Routledge. https://doi.org/10.4324/9781315167305

Calzada, I. (2021). Data co-operatives through data sovereignty. *Smart Cities, 4*(3), 1158–1172. https://doi.org/10.3390/smartcities4030062

Carmi, E., Yates, S. J., Lockley, E., & Pawluczuk, A. (2020). Data citizenship: Rethinking data literacy in the age of disinformation, misinformation, and malinformation. *Internet Policy Review, 9*(2). https://doi.org/10.14763/2020.2.1481

Carroll, S. R., Garba, I., Figueroa-Rodríguez, O. L., Holbrook, J., Lovett, R., Materechera, S., Parsons, M., Raseroka, K., Rodriguez-Lonebear, D., Rowe, R., Sara, R., Walker, J. D., Anderson, J., & Hudson, M. (2020). The CARE principles for indigenous data governance. *Data Science Journal, 19*(1), 43. https://doi.org/10.5334/dsj-2020-043

Cohen, M., Rohan, A., Pritchard, K., & Pettit, K. (2022). *Guide to data chats: Convening community conversations about data.* Urban Institute. Retrieved July 15, 2022, from https://www.urban.org/research/publication/guide-data-chats-convening-community-conversations-about-data

Criado-Perez, C. (2019). *Invisible women: Exposing data bias in a world designed for men.* Abrams Press.

D'Ignazio, C., & Bhargava, R. (2015). *Approaches to building big data literacy.* Bloomberg Data for Good Exchange Conference 2015. Retrieved April 4, 2022, from https://www.media.mit.edu/publications/approaches-to-building-big-data-literacy/

Dawson McGuinness, T., & Schank, H. (2021). *Power to the public: The promise of public interest technology.* Princeton University Press.

Eubanks, V. (2018). *Automating inequality: How high-tech tools profile, police, and punish the poor.* St. Martin's Press.

European Parliament, & the Council of the European Union. (2016). REGULATION (EU) 2016/679 OF THE EUROPEAN PARLIAMENT AND OF THE COUNCIL of 27 April 2016 on the protection of natural persons with regard to the processing of personal data and on the free movement of such data, and repealing Directive 95/46/EC (General Data Protection Regulation). *Official Journal of the European Union,* L199/1–L119/88. Retrieved April 7, 2022, from https://eur-lex.europa.eu/eli/reg/2016/679/oj

Farmer, J., McCosker, A., Kamstra, P., Perkins, D., Dalton, H., Powell, N., Salvador-Carulla, L., Bagheri, N., Bishop, L., Gardiner, F., Greco, M., Smith J., Hislop, C., Somerville, R., Blanchard, M., Potter, S., Banks, C., & Starling, M. (2020). *Mapping the hidden voices in rural mental health: A pilot study of online community data*. Swinburne University of Technology. Retrieved April 4, 2022, from https://apo.org.au/node/303092

Flowing Data. (2013). *Data hackathon challenges and why questions are important*. Retrieved April 4, 2022, from https://flowingdata.com/2013/03/12/data-hackathon-challenges-and-why-questions-are-important/

Frank, M., Walker, J., Attard, J., & Tygel, A. (2016). Data literacy – What is it and how can we make it happen? *The Journal of Community Informatics, 12*(3), 4–8. https://doi.org/10.15353/joci.v12i3.3274

Gregory, A. G., & Howard, D. (2009). The nonprofit starvation cycle. *Stanford Social Innovation Review, 7*(4), 49–53. https://doi.org/10.48558/6K3V-0Q70

Grzymek, V., & Puntschuh, M. (2019). Was Europa über algorithmen weiß und denkt: Ergebnisse einer repräsentativen Bevölkerungsumfrage Impuls Algorithmenethik. *Bertelsmann Stiftung*. https://doi.org/10.11586/2019006

Henriques-Gomes, L. (2020, May 29). Robodebt: Government to refund 470,000 unlawful Centrelink debts worth $721m. *The Guardian*. Retrieved April 4, 2022 from https://www.theguardian.com/australia-news/2020/may/29/robodebt-government-to-repay-470000-unlawful-centrelink-debts-worth-721m

Incite! Women of Color Against Violence. (2017). *The revolution will not be funded: Beyond the non-profit industrial complex*. Duke University Press.

Infoxchange. (2020). *Digital technology in the not-for-profit sector*. Retrieved April 4, 2022, from https://www.infoxchange.org/sites/default/files/digital_technology_in_the_not-for-profit_sector_2020.pdf

Kamstra, P., Farmer, J., McCosker, A., Gardiner, F., Dalton, H., Perkins, D., Salvador-Carulla, L., & Bagheri, N. (in press). A novel mixed method approach for integrating Not-for-profit service data via qualitative GIS to explore authentic experiences of ill-health: A case study of rural mental health. *Journal of Mixed Methods Research*.

Kukutai, T., & Taylor, J. (2016). *Indigenous data sovereignty: Toward an agenda*. ANU Press.

Lalande, L. (2018). *Peering into the future: Reimagining governance in the nonprofit sector* (Mowat Research No. 171). The Mowat Centre. Retrieved April 4, 2022, from https://munkschool.utoronto.ca/mowatcentre/peering-into-the-future/

Lalande, L., & Cave, J. (2017). *Measuring outcomes in practice: Fostering an enabling environment for measurement in Canada* (Mowat Research No. 157). The Mowat Centre. Retrieved April 4, 2022, from https://munkschool.utoronto.ca/mowatcentre/measuring-outcomes-in-practice/

LeChasseur, K. (2016). Re-examining power and privilege in collective impact. *Community Development, 47*(2), 225–240. https://doi.org/10.1080/15575330.2016.1140664

Loukissas, Y. A. (2019). *All data are local: Thinking critically in a data-driven society*. MIT Press.

Müller-Peters, H. (2020). Big data: Chancen und Risiken aus Sicht der Bürger. In S. Knorre, H. Müller-Peters, & F. Wagner (Eds.), *Die big-data-debatte: Chancen und Risiken der Digital Vernetzten Gesellschaft* (pp. 137–193). Springer.

Murray, B., Falkenberger, E., & Saxena, P. (2015). *Data walks: An innovative way to share data with communities*. Urban Institute. Retrieved April 4, 2022, from https://www.urban.org/research/publication/data-walks-innovative-way-share-data-communities

Noble, S. U. (2018). *Algorithms of oppression*. New York University Press.

O'Neil, C. (2016). *Weapons of math destruction: How big data increases inequality and threatens democracy*. Crown Publishing Group.

O'Neil, C., & Schutt, R. (2013). *Doing data science: Straight talk from the frontline*. O'Reilly Media.

Picciano, A. G. (2012). The evolution of big data and learning analytics in American higher education. *Journal of Asynchronous Learning Networks, 16*(3). https://doi.org/10.24059/olj.v16i3.267

Piff, J. (2021). Data in collective impact: Focusing on what matters. *Stanford Social Innovation Review*. https://doi.org/10.48558/9c8p-wd91

Productivity Commission. (2010). *Contribution of the not-for-profit sector: Productivity Commission research report*. Retrieved April 4, 2022, from https://www.pc.gov.au/inquiries/completed/not-for-profit/report

Sainty, E. (2019, April 30). Social impact bonds: A letter from the frontline. *SVA Quarterly*. Retrieved April 7, 2022, from https://www.socialventures.com.au/sva-quarterly/social-impact-bonds-a-letter-from-the-frontline-part1/

Salamon, L. M. (2014). *New frontiers of philanthropy: A guide to the new tools and actors reshaping global philanthropy and social investing*. Oxford University Press.

Salamon, L. M., & Sokolowski, W. (2018). The size and composition of the European third sector. In B. Enjolras, L. M. Salamon, K. H. Sivesind, &

A. Zimmer (Eds.), *The third sector as a renewable resource for Europe* (pp. 49–93). Palgrave Macmillan.

Sander, I. (2020). Critical big data literacy tools—Engaging citizens and promoting empowered internet usage. *Data & Policy, 2*, e5. https://doi.org/10.1017/dap.2020.5

Social Ventures Australia. (2021). *Managing to outcomes: A guide to developing an outcomes focus.* Retrieved April 4, 2022, from https://www.socialventures.com.au/assets/SVA-Outcomes-Management-Guide.pdf

Social Ventures Australia and the Centre for Social Impact. (2021). *Vital support: Building resilient charities to support Australia's wellbeing.* Retrieved April 7, 2022, from https://www.socialventures.com.au/work/vital-support-building-resilient-charities-to-support-australias-wellbeing/

Srnicek, N. (2016). *Platform capitalism*. Wiley.

Susha, I., Janssen, M., & Verhulst, S. (2017). Data collaboratives as a new frontier of cross-sector partnerships in the age of open data: Taxonomy development. *Proceedings of the 50th Hawaii International Conference on System Sciences 2017*, Waikoloa Village, Hawaii, United States. https://doi.org/10.24251/HICSS.2017.325

Tennant, M., Sanders, J., O'Brien, M., & Castle, C. (2006). *Defining the non-profit sector: New Zealand* (Johns Hopkins Comparative Nonprofit Sector Project, Working Paper No. 45). The Johns Hopkins Center for Civil Society Studies.

Tripp, W., Gage, D., & Williams, H. (2020). Addressing the data analytics gap: A community university partnership to enhance analytics capabilities in the non-profit sector. *Collaborations: A Journal of Community-Based Research and Practice, 3*(1), 11. https://doi.org/10.33596/coll.58

van Zoonen, L. (2020). Data governance and citizen participation in the digital welfare state. *Data & Policy, 2*, e10. https://doi.org/10.1017/dap.2020.10

Vaughan, S. K., & Arsneault, S. (2013). *Managing nonprofit organizations in a policy world.* CQ Press.

Verhulst, S., & Young, A. (2017). The potential of social media intelligence to improve people's lives: Social media data for good. *The Governance Lab.* Retrieved April 7, 2022, from https://papers.ssrn.com/sol3/papers.cfm?abstract_id=3141457

Verhulst, S. G. (2021). Reimagining data responsibility: 10 new approaches toward a culture of trust in re-using data to address critical public needs. *Data & Policy, 3*, e6. https://doi.org/10.1017/dap.2021.4

Warne, H., Dencik, L., & Hintz, A. (2021). Advancing civic participation in algorithmic decision-making: A guidebook for the public sector. *Data Justice Lab*. Retrieved April 7, 2022, from https://orca.cardiff.ac.uk/143384/

Williams, S. (2020). *Data action: Using data for public good*. MIT Press.

Wilson, E., Campain, R., & Brown, C. D. (2021). *The community services outcomes tree. An introduction.* Centre for Social Impact, Swinburne University of Technology. https://doi.org/10.25916/7e8f-dm74

Open Access This chapter is licensed under the terms of the Creative Commons Attribution 4.0 International License (http://creativecommons.org/licenses/by/4.0/), which permits use, sharing, adaptation, distribution and reproduction in any medium or format, as long as you give appropriate credit to the original author(s) and the source, provide a link to the Creative Commons licence and indicate if changes were made.

The images or other third party material in this chapter are included in the chapter's Creative Commons licence, unless indicated otherwise in a credit line to the material. If material is not included in the chapter's Creative Commons licence and your intended use is not permitted by statutory regulation or exceeds the permitted use, you will need to obtain permission directly from the copyright holder.

2

Case Studies of Data Projects

Chapter 1 made the case for non-profits building their data capability as part of enabling their work for social good. This chapter jumps straight into the reality of how organisations start to work with different types of datasets and learn about working with data. We present three case studies of our own research working with different non-profit (and other) organisations and different internal re-used datasets, as well as open public datasets. Each case study features collaborative data action and—we argue—results in steps towards data capability. We jump straight to the projects here because this is really what happened in our work. We took our skillsets from our different research backgrounds—approximately data science, communications and community development—and looked at how we could partner with organisations to address their real challenges. As well as having a problem to solve, each partner organisation we worked with also had a curiosity to find out about whether data science could help. In our first case study, we worked with government departments and agencies to understand the public conversation on family violence and the impact of policy. For the second, we partnered with three non-profits looking to solve social problems with data. Our final case study is a collaboration with several community organisations and a bank in a regional city. The case studies illustrate the evolution of our work with data over 2017–2021, and how we came to arrive at collaborative data action as a methodology as it was trialled and refined over a series of studies. There are hints about what building data capability involves in each case study, but we only started to build in processes of evaluation as our studies progressed. Hence, the case studies have slightly different formats. And only over this evolution of cases and other data projects have we arrived at our understanding of data capability. This is explored in Chap. 3.

We suggest the case studies show how data projects that involve social mission-driven organisations benefit from combining multiple skills and perspectives. This is because applying data science in domains of social action is complex. It benefits from knowledge of relevant evidence, acknowledging that ideology and values are always present, and above all it benefits from practitioner expertise through their experience working in contexts that highlight what is significant and how to address it. Our case studies are light-on regarding the techniques of 'big data' science because this is not a book on how to do data analytics technically. That is covered in other texts (e.g., Aragon et al., 2022). In this chapter, we focus more on *what we did* from an operational, indeed co-operational, standpoint. We expand on what that means—the implications and how to build data capability—more in Chaps. 3 and 4. Case study projects 2 and 3 took place during 2020–2021 during the COVID-19 pandemic when extended lockdowns meant a lack of face-to-face engagement. The case studies are as follows:

The project featured in Case Study 1 involved re-using data for insights into the public conversation about family violence following implementation of new state family violence policy. Working mainly with a government department concerned with family violence policy, but also in consultations with non-profit stakeholders, the case study addresses how to gain information about social outcomes by re-using qualitative datasets generated via social media and public consultation. It thus exemplifies some of the kinds of datasets, analyses and visualisations that non-profits could use when looking for novel data to inform outcomes evaluation.

The project in Case Study 2 involved working with three non-profits of different sizes. They partnered to learn if and how they could use internal already-generated data to create added value, particularly around showing their organisations' direct and wider social impacts and, on the other hand, to improve organisational effectiveness.

Case Study 3 illustrates how seven organisations, including non-profits and a bank, worked together to find out if and how they could use their internal data, plus open data, to find out more about their community. They brought data together to generate geospatially visualised data layers describing community resilience, including layers about social connection, financial wellbeing, homelessness and housing, and demand for social services. The case highlights some of the potential and challenges in sharing data amongst organisations.

Table 2.1 summarises the case studies including an overview of the topic and nature of the collaboration, datasets used, analyses and visualisations and key learnings.

At the end of this chapter, we compare some aspects across the cases, mainly considering what was learned as this informs the themes about building capability and collaboration that are extended in Chap. 3.

Case Study 1: Outcomes of Family Violence Policy—A Public Sector Collaboration

Project Goal

Explore the value of novel datasets to inform the State Government of Victoria, Australia, about changes to the public conversation after it introduced new policies to address family violence.

Project Description

The Victorian Government produced new family violence prevention policies in 2017 in response to a Royal Commission investigation (2015–2016). Alongside recommendations for public and community sector reform, the government produced a framework of outcome indicators. These tended to reflect aspirations for change and were considered

Table 2.1 Summary data projects case comparison

Topic and collaboration	Data	Analyses/ visualisations	Key learning
Case 1: Family violence policy outcomes. Multiple government agencies and non-profits	*Internal data*: Consultation submissions *External data*: Twitter, Media reporting data	Timelines, topics volume of topics over time, influential people and organisations	Participants found new insights to inform policy outcomes and developed greater confidence with using data
Case 2: Re-using operational data. Multiple departments and staff of three non-profits	*Internal data*: Operational datasets about staff and service locations, employee training, journeys, surveys *External data*: Government open data, City environmental reports	Graphs, geospatial journey visualisations	Participants felt more in control and knowledgeable that they could use operational data for strategy and impact evaluation
Case 3: Community resilience indicators data collaborative. Multiple organisations in a regional city	*Internal data*: Surveys, housing and service locations, customer data *External data*: Government open data	Interactive data dashboard with geospatial (map) visualisations by suburb, graphs and pie charts	Participants developed confidence about using data, critique of practices and challenges. They developed relationships of trust and learned about each other's work

difficult to measure, particularly those related to improved awareness, understanding and attitudes about family violence in the community. Some of the outcomes were complicated to assess; for example, while the policy sought a "reduction in all family violence behaviours" (State Government of Victoria, n.d., p. 6), family violence incident reporting rose, possibly because people were more comfortable with coming forward and were supported to do so with better services. Simply measuring changes in crime statistics, therefore, gave potentially misleading results.

We worked with government and government agency partners to target outcomes relating to changes in public discussion. We assessed changes by analysing: (a) the public consultation submissions that informed the new policy (to establish a baseline of core family violence issues) collected in 2015 and (b) public discussion through social media data (Twitter) and news media reporting to understand how the public conversation changed in response to public policy during 2014–2018.

Collaborating Partners

The project was instigated by the Victorian Department of Premier and Cabinet (DPC). The DPC leads the whole of Victoria state government policy and performance, coordinating activities to help the government achieve its strategic objectives.

Other partners that collaborated on this project were:

- *Women Victoria*, a state government department promoting gender equality and women's leadership.
- *Respect Victoria*, an agency funded by but independent of state government, dedicated to the primary prevention of all forms of family violence and violence against women.
- *Family Violence Branch* at the Department of Premier and Cabinet, Victorian Government.
- *Family Safety Victoria*, the Victorian Government agency leading the implementation of family violence reforms.
- *Business Insights Unit* at the Department of Premier and Cabinet, Victorian Government.
- *Social Data Analytics Lab* at Swinburne University of Technology.

How the Project Began

The project started with discussions with the DPC in mid-2018 about the feasibility of re-using external data sources to inform outcomes. This was an exploratory project and, as a first step, our DPC partners spent several months identifying a suitable topic and group of stakeholders. Criteria for selection were as follows: that it should be a non-controversial topic area; there should be pre-existing good relationships between relevant agencies and departments; and stakeholders were open to novel data analytics. The DPC had its own Business Insights Unit that analysed data, so these staff were involved with the aim of complementing, not replicating, the work they were already doing. Initial workshops were held involving our multi-disciplinary university researcher team and partner staff, and this led to identifying data sources and likely useful types of analysis.

Summary of Datasets Used

Data sources (see Table 2.2) were selected to provide insights into public discussions about family violence over the five-year study period, allowing comparisons year by year.

Table 2.2 Data sources for public discussion of family violence

Topic	Source	Datasets	Open public or re-used internal data
Informed public and policy documents	Royal Commission into Family Violence public submissions	838 public submissions; we used a stratified sample of 105 submissions	Re-used
Public discussion	Twitter, #familyviolence, #domesticviolence	99,840 Twitter posts from 2819 geographically dispersed Australian Twitter users	Open public
Public discourse	Australian news media, via MIT Media Cloud platform	11,451 news articles from Australian national and regional news sources (including newspapers, radio and TV)	Open public

Methods

Discussion Workshops A steering group with representatives of project partners met six times during the project. Early workshops established questions to pursue in the data analysis and identified a timeline of policy events from 2014. As data was analysed—and explored through subsequent workshops—the group gave feedback on findings and input to aid further analysis. Through these workshops, a *collaborative analysis* strategy was developed.

Data Analysis Data analysis techniques were chosen to fit datasets and project goals. To discover semantic patterns within the large bodies of text data from the three datasets, natural language processing (NLP) was used to augment qualitative content and thematic analysis. This involved word frequency and clustering analysis, using Pearson Coefficient Correlation analysis (Pearson's r), and the topic modelling method Latent Dirichlet Allocation (LDA). The approach to analysis is informed by established theory in policy analysis, frame analysis and socio-linguistics that addresses the formation of public social issues and understands the role of language and communication in 'framing' or shaping and contesting the parameters of those issues.

A timeline analysis of the Twitter dataset identified peaks in discussion across the five-year timeframe and matched these with known policy or public events. Named entity recognition was also used to identify key individuals and organisations and their prominence at different times.

Submissions to the Royal Commission Public Inquiry (2015) The sample of public submissions was analysed using word frequency and thematic clustering, as well as qualitative content analysis to establish a baseline of the key policy dimensions framing family violence. The submissions were taken as a proxy for the attitudes and topics discussed by an *informed public*—that is, the diverse individuals, community sector and services, government and research voices, who have experiences of family violence or work with victim survivors or perpetrators.

Twitter Corpus (January 2014–December 2018) To identify topics in the Twitter dataset over the target timeframe, a sampling strategy was used, generating a maximum of 500 tweets per week. To inform the timeline analysis, this sample was supplemented by extracting the *Twitter counts endpoint* which returns the total tweet count at each timepoint. This allows quantification of tweets beyond the 500 per week sample.

LDA topic modelling was applied to Twitter posts for each year. Since LDA is an unsupervised learning model, there is no ground-truth on the number of topics, and therefore it is the researcher's responsibility to validate the appropriate number of topic clusters. For our study, the number of topics identified for each year is established by model parameter checks. The topic modelling process established a range of topic options, and these were reviewed by the researchers on the team to identify the most coherent and distinct topics, with the number of topics varying each year.

News Media Corpus (January 2014–December 2018) The meta-data captured via the API for each article included the source name (media outlet), time and date of the article. We cleaned the media dataset by scraping the body of the articles from provided links. Stories with invalid URL links and duplicate stories published in more than one outlet were removed, retaining the first published article. LDA topic modelling was applied to the news media corpus, and a hand-annotated topic descriptor was associated with each cluster.

With all the datasets, reliability of machine analysis was checked by manual qualitative coding of samples of data items (tweets, stories and public submissions) and inter-coder reliability checks involving four people independently coding samples. The team checked emergent topics against the outcomes framework we were seeking to inform, existing research evidence and the Royal Commission reports.

Findings

We reported a range of findings that helped identify the longer-term changes in the way family violence was discussed and were able to estimate the main effects of the Royal Commission and subsequent policy initiatives. These changes, observable through the different public discourse datasets (news, Twitter, public inquiry submissions), were mapped against the government's official outcome indicators. A number of diagrams and chart types were chosen to present the most salient findings. These choices matter, and working with large corpus natural language or text datasets meant that innovative techniques had to be used to convey findings concisely and dynamically.

A *tree diagram* was used to visualise five core thematic dimensions of family violence identified through analysis of the Royal Commission public submissions and policy reports, which were victims, perpetrators, causes and contexts, systems, and solutions. These dimensions served as a baseline and were used to compare changes to the public conversation thereafter.

Two *standard graphs* were used to quantify public discussion of family violence, and show change over time, against the five Royal Commission dimensions. This revealed alignment and divergence between public discourse and policy frameworks.

Two *ribbon graphs* (see Fig. 2.1) were used to represent and quantify the change in news media and Twitter topics, between 2014 and 2018, and the continuity and discontinuity of those topics. We drew out insights from this analysis. For example, in Twitter data, victim survivors and perpetrators are discussed more directly and pointedly, and victim survivors voice their own experiences, to a far greater extent than in news media and policy reports and inquiry submissions. At a high level, we showed that the public conversation changed in relation to the 2015 hearings of the Royal Commission and policy framing. Unlike Twitter, which consistently followed the hearings and amplified the issues it raised, news media reporting was much slower to change or respond to the Royal Commission. The news coverage only took off with the rise of the #MeToo movement in late 2018.

A *Twitter timeline graph* identified key public events against peaks and troughs in Twitter activity (Fig. 2.2). This helped to discover when there was attention to key policy events and other influential public actions and controversies.

Bubble charts were also used, drawing on named entity analysis, which quantifies mentions of people or organisations in the data. This showed the relationship between Twitter and news media items by key topic area and influential people and organisations. These changed over time.

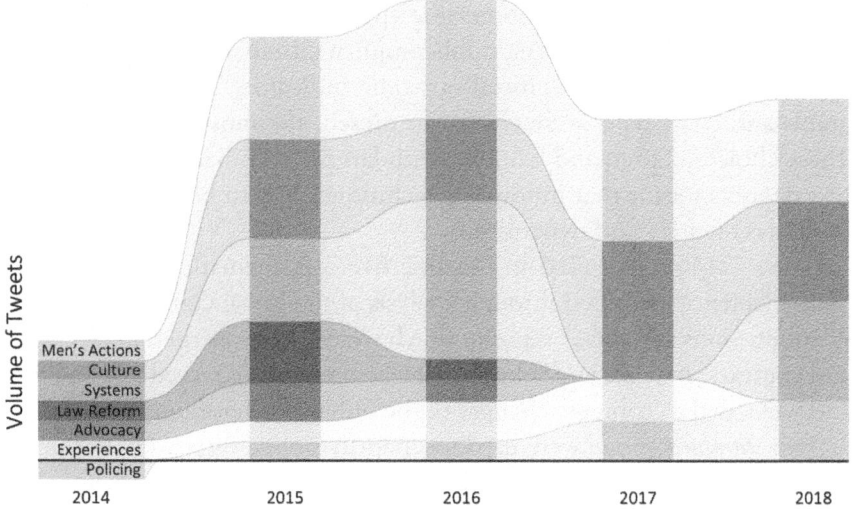

Fig. 2.1 Topic modelling analysis of Twitter topics related to family violence 2014–2018. *Note*: Ribbon graph adapted from data in "Community responses to family violence: Charting policy outcomes using novel data sources, text mining and topic modelling". by A. McCosker, J. Farmer, and A. Soltani Panah, 2020, *Swinburne University of Technology*, p. 24, https://apo.org.au/sites/default/files/resource-files/2020-03/apo-nid278041.pdf. (Copyright 2020 by Swinburne University of Technology. Adapted with permission)

Through the named entity analysis, we identified key players in the public debates surrounding family violence over the target period. This included politicians, advocates and activists, as well as news organisations.

Outcomes and Lessons Learned

The data analysis gave fresh insights relating to how family violence was discussed and changes over time post-policy change. It showed the DPC that there were datasets that could inform their outcomes about public attitude and public discussion changes. Where they had previously relied on community surveys that tend to feature limited demographics in response, by re-using other datasets they could access a wider range of attitudes and language. Analysis raised new issues that they had not thought about previously, such as what topics were featured in policy

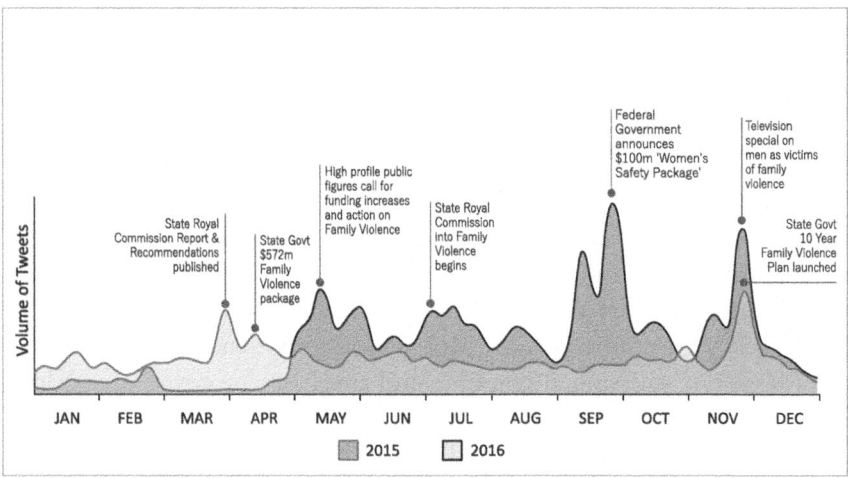

Fig. 2.2 Timeline and peaks of Twitter activity addressing family violence by year (2015 and 2016 represented). Note: Twitter timeline analysis graph adapted from data in "Community responses to family violence: Charting policy outcomes using novel data sources, text mining and topic modelling". by A. McCosker, J. Farmer, and A. Soltani Panah, 2020, *Swinburne University of Technology*, p. 29, https://apo.org.au/sites/default/files/resource-files/2020-03/apo-nid278041.pdf. (Copyright 2020 by Swinburne University of Technology. Adapted with permission)

compared with public concerns. For example, there was limited and abstract discussion of perpetrators, but as time passed, there was more nuanced discussion on Twitter about men as perpetrators and social and structural factors influencing family violence. That the news media continued sensationalising tropes about violence showed that government still needed to do more to influence news media reporting. They found out that the public uses different and diverse words (compared to policy) to depict and discuss forms of family violence, particularly using the term 'abuse'. An evolving timeline of public responses highlighted that policy events influenced volume and duration of peaks in Twitter discussion more than some very serious crime events. Analyses also highlighted how particular people and organisations influence the conversation in different directions. Together, the analyses gave a much more nuanced perspective about how the public responds to policy that could inform useful changes to policy over time.

The project featured collaborative research around evaluating outcomes in relation to a significant social policy issue with government departments and arms-length agencies. As such, it showed that through collaborating to bring multiple knowledges and skills to the table, existing data could be re-used to find evidence, rather than collecting new data. We introduced new types of data and analytical methods and showed how partners' current social media analysis could be refined and extended.

The work led to our research team developing ongoing relationships with the departments and agencies. Specifically, it also led to a presentation at a key government knowledge transfer event and to newly funded research about accessing, integrating and analysing the government's longitudinal datasets on family violence.

Re-using data and using novel data analytics techniques is challenging, and in large, traditional, bureaucratic organisations requires determined champions to drive experimentation and change. While we were fortunate to work with a series of senior advocates within government, the project was hampered by multiple senior staff changes throughout the study period, affecting continuity, support and understanding of the work.

The collaborative processes we used may appear time-intensive, but they offer substantial methodological benefits from bringing in different expertise, perspectives and questions and achieve direct impact in influencing knowledge and awareness about data amongst those that participate. Potentially, these representatives are inspired to return to their departments and agencies and be more confident about advocating for using data and growing skills in data use.

For further information about the project see McCosker et al. (2020).

Case Study 2: Re-using Operational Data with Three Non-Profits

Project Goal

Explore the relevance and feasibility of data analytics for non-profits through deploying a collaborative data action methodology.

Project Description

Australian non-profits are aware of the rise of the data analytics movement, but many lack the capability and resources that would allow them to fully utilise their data via analytics. The three non-profit partners in this project provide services for different target groups and have different existing requirements to use data—including to report to external funders and government regulators. Each has gathered a set of datasets over a number of years in relation to their work.

We facilitated a series of iterative workshops with staff to identify their organisational 'pain points' (i.e., problems and questions), understand their datasets and determine if and how data analytics could be used to provide new insights that could guide future strategies. We also developed a series of educational webinars about working with data, including information on relevant laws, local policies, technological tools and open data portals. Non-profits' staff were interviewed at the beginning of the project to assess aspects of their existing organisational data capability and their hopes and expectations. Interviews were repeated at the end of the project to discover benefits and reflect on learning and challenges.

The project ran from 2020 to early 2021. While originally we envisaged multiple face-to-face meetings and training sessions, ultimately all sessions were conducted online. Both non-profits' staff and researchers spent several months in lockdown due to the COVID-19 pandemic and dealt with multiple operational challenges while they participated in the project.

Collaborating Partners

The project was funded by the *Lord Mayors Charitable Foundation* (LMCF) (a philanthropic foundation based in Melbourne), the non-profit organisations that participated, and a small grant from our university. The non-profit partners were:

1. *Yooralla,* an organisation providing services for people with disabilities in their homes and the community.

2. *Good Cycles,* a social enterprise that provides supported employment for young people who might otherwise have difficulty accessing jobs and training due to social and economic disadvantage. Good Cycles engages young people in work experience including in operating retail bicycle shops, mobile car share cleaning, bike share, and parcel deliveries and logistics—all using cargo bikes instead of cars or trucks. In addition to providing training and employment, the organisation promotes urban sustainability.
3. *Entertainment Assist,* a charity that raises awareness about mental health and wellbeing in workplaces and for employees in the Australian entertainment industry. Entertainment Assist offers a mental health training programme (*Intermission*) for staff and employers.

How the Project Began

Leaders at the LMCF partnered with our team because they were interested to explore the potential of new capabilities in understanding and using data from partnering with a university data lab to find, examine, analyse and visualise data.

Once initial partial funding from LMCF was secured, the next step was to identify and attract three or four non-profits that would also co-fund their participation. Establishing agreement from the non-profits to participate sometimes took several conversations over two to three months, involving researchers, non-profit managers and staff. The researchers shared examples from past data projects, as well as gave examples from initiatives like The GovLab (https://datacollaboratives.org) and NESTA UK's data analytics projects and reports. While there was strong initial interest from potential partners, negotiating to the point of securing participation and funding was a significant challenge. As the COVID-19 pandemic hit, one partner (a large community health service provider) was forced to withdraw to focus on core business.

Summary of Datasets Used

We focused on re-using non-profit partners' internal datasets but drew on open public datasets to support and complement these datasets, helping to produce new insights (Table 2.3).

Table 2.3 Datasets used in the three non-profits' analyses

Non-profit organisation/topic	Source	Datasets	Open public data or re-used internal data
Entertainment Assist/impacts on mental health and wider social impact	*Intermission* evaluation survey data	Participant responses to mental health training by demographics	Re-used
	Australian Bureau of Statistics	National Survey of Mental Health and Wellbeing: Summary of results, 2008	Open public
Good Cycles/worker skills development, social and environmental impact	Transitional Employment Programme data	Geospatial data about trainees' bicycle journeys while delivering services	Re-used
	City of Melbourne Transport Strategy 2030	Congestion, emissions and health outcomes related to transport	Open public
Yooralla/employee wellbeing and retention	Human resources and training data	Staff travel to work, during work and training data	Re-used
	Australian Bureau of Statistics	Data by Region, Population and People levels of post-secondary school qualifications and median levels of general population employee income across Melbourne 2014–2019	Open public

Methods

Educational Webinar Series A webinar series was designed aiming to familiarise non-profit partners' staff with foundational concepts about data analytics in the context of their sector. Five webinars were pre-recorded by the research team and distributed via email weblink, with supporting resources and recommended readings. Webinars ran concurrently with the co-design workshops from August to November 2020. Topics covered included introducing data projects, data ethics and governance, data collaborative methodologies, sharing a technology toolkit and next steps in organisational data analytics. A final interactive webinar was conducted via Zoom in February 2021, bringing non-profit staff participants and the university team together to share project findings and insights.

Discussion Workshops Staff from each non-profit participated in three data analytics workshops specifically exploring their questions and data. The workshops covered the following:

Workshop 1: Goals of the project, key 'pain-points' and questions, and identifying internal datasets;
Workshop 2: Review and discussion of initial data analyses and visualisations;
Workshop 3: 'Deeper dives' into organisational data visualisations, use of other open public datasets to enrich analyses and discussion of how to communicate and apply data analyses.

The non-profits were responsible for identifying relevant internal datasets and ensuring these were de-identified according to the Australian *Privacy Act 1988*. These datasets were shared with Swinburne researchers via SharePoint (a secure enterprise file-sharing platform).

Following workshops 1 and 2, the research team's data scientists worked with non-profits' staff to generate visualisations based on partners' internal datasets. Following workshop 3, some open public data sources were analysed and visualised to compare or add value to internal data analyses. These processes involving non-profit staff in processes of cleaning, obtaining, analysing and visualising data provided opportunities for non-profit staff to identify potential value from data analytics as well as to understand the work, technologies and governance issues involved. Collaborative working between university and non-profits' staff inspired discussions about future investments in data science capability-building for their organisations.

The workshop approach drew on aspects of the *data walk* method pioneered by the Washington DC based Urban Institute (Murray et al., 2015). This method focuses on visualising data and sharing and discussing visualisations as a method of collaboration, participation and iteratively honing analyses to address participants' questions.

Data Analysis

Entertainment Assist Data scientists from the research team worked with Entertainment Assist to generate several different visualisations using the *Intermission* course evaluation survey data. Descriptive statistics and sentiment analysis were applied. In workshop discussions, differences between managers and staff cohorts undertaking the training were identified, and this drove a next round of data analysis further exploring the responses from these groups. Workshop 3 raised the idea of comparing programme participants by job, as those taking the course range from young performing artists to older technical staff. Word clouds, sentiment analysis and other types of statistical analyses compared data from the Intermission dataset with data from the Australian Bureau of Statistics' Australian National Survey of Mental Health and Wellbeing. The comparison generated new insights about the potential impacts of the Intermission programme for particular at-risk cohorts as highlighted by national data.

Good Cycles Data about training by employee from the Transitional Employment Program dataset was initially used to generate an analysis of tracking workers' progress in building employment skills over time. Thereafter, worker journey data was used to generate a geospatial visualisation of data showing 2514 trainees' bicycle journeys during the course of service delivery over three months. Bicycle journeys were visualised as trails on a map of Melbourne's suburbs.

Building on these initial analyses, geospatial data about trainee journeys from Good Cycles facilities to customer sites was compared with environmental modelling data from the City of Melbourne Transport Strategy 2030 (City of Melbourne, 2020) to help calculate the environmental benefits, in terms of reduced traffic congestion, reduced carbon emissions and improved citizen health outcomes, of employees travelling by bicycle as opposed to car or truck.

Yooralla Yooralla was interested to improve staff experiences of work, and analysis began by examining internal operational human resources and training datasets. Geospatial and temporal visualisations were initially generated, showing aggregated data about staff demographics, rostering history and training by Yooralla service location. Thereafter, an objective became to discover variables linked to staff retention, and one target suggested to explore was to compare staff demographics with distances travelled to reach workplaces. A key question pursued was—might distance travelled to their workplace influence staff retention?

For discussion at workshop 3, datasets analysed included Australian Bureau of Statistics (ABS) data about median levels of general population employee income across Melbourne, compared with geospatial postcode data for Yooralla employees and geospatial postcode data about employees' primary workplace (ABS, 2020a). Datasets were compared for any insights relating to associations between median income for suburbs and staff home and work locations.

Findings

Insights from Data Analyses Each non-profit participated in generating analyses and visualisations that they considered helpful in understanding and explaining the challenges they brought to the project. As examples, staff of Entertainment Assist were able to better understand the significance of their training course for particular target groups and to consider how training might be tailored for different groups. For example, young, mostly female dance students and stagehands who are mostly middle-aged men would both be key target groups but would need differently configured training content.

Data analysis and visualisations generated allowed Good Cycles to demonstrate their contribution to the environmental sustainability of Greater Melbourne because the impact of employees' travel by bicycle could be calculated in terms of impact on congestion, emissions and public health. Figure 2.3 provides an indication of how Good Cycles' employees journey data can be shown. This particular depiction selects out only three cycling employees' journeys across Melbourne from the Good Cycles' depot but serves to show the type of geospatial visualisation that Good Cycles found useful.

Insights for Yooralla included understanding the impact of the locations of their service hubs (often in higher income suburbs) in relation to where

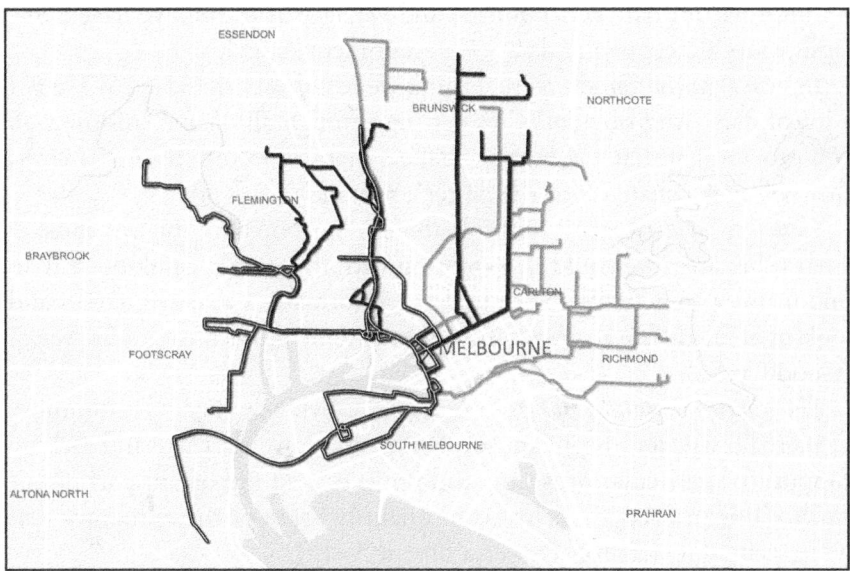

Fig. 2.3 Geospatial visualisation of three Good Cycles' employee journeys

their staff could afford to live (a majority resided in mid-lower income suburbs). Disparities meant staff had long journeys to work and this potentially related to staff retention. Through a visualisation of internal and ABS employment and income datasets, Yooralla saw that the average daily commute for their employees was nearly 60 km return journey. This is considerably further than the average Australian commuting distance (ABS, 2020b). This led the Yooralla team to consider whether new work practices and staff work locations could be significant when trying to improve staff retention. Insights generated from the work ultimately led Yooralla to develop new policies for employee rostering.

From the Before and After Interviews

The non-profits' managers shared their initial goals for participating in interviews held at the start of the project. The main themes are summarised below, with illustrative quotes.

Improve organisational data know-how: "The best-case outcome is that … we improve our definitions, we improve our measurement, and we improve our data collection … and we have a culture, we have a discipline around capturing data" (Entertainment Assist).

Inform organisation strategy: "I think we've got very rich data. We've got a lot of data. And obviously, it's getting through all of that information and providing it that will inform change, that will inform improvements, that will make changes for the better"(Yooralla).

Generate new insights: "I think there is an opportunity…to look at what other areas we could be exploring with this data. I think there is an opportunity to actually look at all the information that we have—and look at it in different ways, and look at it in more meaningful ways" (Good Cycles).

Show outcomes and impacts to funders: "Obviously there are a number of incredibly generous philanthropic organisations out there and seeking support for particular programs and projects is an important part of our work. [This project] … helps us to quantify some of the outcomes that we're seeking to achieve" (Entertainment Assist).

At the end of the project, participants identified immediate benefits from using data visualisations in reports to board members and funding bodies. For example, Good Cycles used a visualisation as part of a competitive tendering process to show the advantages their use of bicycle transport had for the environment:

> [The client] said, 'What's your footprint? What sort of area can we cover?' So, I got [Swinburne data scientist] to send me the heat map ... I packaged that up and we sent that back to the client, to demonstrate how far north of the CBD [Central Business District] we go, how far south-east and west. It was good, it was a valuable piece of data. (Good Cycles)

All participants reported that the iterative workshop discussions of visualised data helped them to understand challenges and impacts associated with using their data which built their skills for working with data. One organisation, for example, realised there was a need to streamline current use of open text in reporting processes to generate more consistent and useful information:

> People would put in the same concept [into the database] in 40 different ways ... [It was] a bit of a wake-up call for us, and it really clarified that there's only five major classifications that we want to look at in terms of risk, and that it's actually easier for us to show what the problems are to stakeholders if we just use five risk classifications. (Yooralla)

Outcomes and Lessons Learned

The project took a long time to start, partly due to challenges of the pandemic and lockdowns, but also because potential partner non-profits were uncertain about committing to participation. In preliminary interviews, staff 'confessed' their lack of formal training in data analytics or their lack of experience with specific tools or resources for managing and visualising data. Some expressed embarrassment about the 'messiness' of their organisation's data. While most participants worked with data to some degree, all assessed their understanding of data practices as limited.

Concern was particularly acute where large volumes of data were already generated. Participants discussed workarounds to deal with poor systems or their lack of know-how. For example, one participant described downloading datasets from the organisation's proprietary human resources software, which they then manually imported into Excel to generate monthly reports.

A key finding from the project was that through collaborating with the university team, non-profit staff and leaders developed a different philosophy of thinking about data. They started to view data, its collection, and stewardship as a resource management issue, with datasets as resources that were useful to them depending on their skills and knowledge around using them. This was a shift from thinking about data as a compliance issue, something they *had to do* to assuage funders and regulators. Non-profit participants started to think about protecting and owning the value in data with an eye to the insights they could glean from different types of analyses.

Despite multiple challenges caused by working during the pandemic and its lockdowns, project aims were met. Unforeseen impacts included participants reporting that working with data sparked new collaboration between internal staff teams that had previously been siloed. This prompted new thinking about ways the combined teams might work with other organisations to combine resources and build data collaborations.

For further information about the project, see Albury et al. (2021).

Case Study 3: City of Greater Bendigo Data Collaborative

Project Goal

Assess the feasibility and potential benefits of a community data collaborative.

Project Description

Place-based planning and collaboration to address community challenges is encouraged in Australian government policy (Government of Victoria, 2020). However, planning for rural places is challenged by lack of data at meaningful spatial levels (Payton Scally et al., 2020). Forming a data collaborative could help by enabling re-use and pooling of data from multiple sources, including non-profits' internal data and open public data. In this project, seven organisations collaborated with university researchers to test the feasibility and potential of pooling and sharing data. The City of Greater Bendigo covers a population of 120,000 living in urban suburbs and rural localities. It is 153 kms (two hours' drive) from central Melbourne, the capital of the state of Victoria, Australia. Working with managers of the partner organisations, the project identified, obtained, analysed and visualised open public datasets and organisations' internal datasets, with mainly geospatial analysis and visualisation by suburbs and localities. During 2021, a series of workshops involving organisation staff and researchers were held to discuss topics of interest, identify datasets, consider useful ways to analyse data and then to discuss mainly geospatially analysed and visualised of datasets. Ultimately, this process informed development of a prototype *community resilience indicator dashboard*.

Collaborating Partners

Partner organisations included a national bank; City of Greater Bendigo council; Haven Home Safe, a non-profit homelessness services provider; Murray Primary Health Network, a government-funded primary health services commissioning organisation; Women's Health Loddon Mallee, a women's health service; and Bendigo Community Health Service and Heathcote Health Service, two community healthcare providers servicing different parts of the City of Greater Bendigo area. Our Swinburne University Social Data Analytics Lab team worked alongside the community partners.

How the Project Began

The project started because a community health service manager was interested in exploring whether a data collaborative could help to overcome lack of data to help assess services' impacts on local health and wellbeing. The manager mobilised a group of other managers of local organisations to form a data collaborative working with our team of data science and social science researchers.

An initial workshop discussed practicalities of data collaboratives and presented examples of international community data initiatives, such as those led by the National Neighborhood Indicators Partnership and The GovLab. Following this, the organisations each contributed to a fund (to an approximate total of US$50,000) to form a data collaborative, and they nominated a lead organisation. Their self-organisation meant the partners committed to work with each other from the start.

As well as an overall contract between the university and the lead organisation, individual data-sharing agreements had to be established between the university and each organisation. We provided a standard template, but each organisation had to generate separately a data-sharing document agreed by their lawyers. This variously took one to five months to organise. As each agreement was signed, we started working with their staff to identify datasets and analyse their data.

While established methodologies about the process of data projects emphasise the need to start with a focused problem or question (GovLab, 2022), our partners found it difficult to identify a specific shared problem. All were interested in community wellbeing and resilience and potentially had datasets that could inform those topics. Consequently, we suggested developing layers of geospatially visualised data, each layer broadly relating to a community resilience topic. Given the partner organisations, the topic-focused data layers we suggested were social connection/isolation, caring, financial wellbeing, housing/homelessness and community health service use.

Summary of Datasets Used

We used open public datasets as well as re-using partners' internal datasets, as Table 2.4 shows.

Methods

Discussion Workshops Six workshops of organisation representatives were held at key stages. Early workshops established organisations' missions, topics of interest and relevant datasets. Discussions with organisations were ongoing between workshops, particularly about establishing

Table 2.4 Datasets for community resilience data collaborative

Topic	Source	Datasets (examples only)	Open public data or re-used internal data
Social connection	Australian Bureau of Statistics (ABS) 2016 Census	Cohorts at risk of social isolation (e.g., men >65 living alone)	Open public
Financial wellbeing	Bank	Relative savings by suburb Government benefits payments by suburb	Re-used
	Council Population Wellbeing Survey	Perceived financial wellbeing Food security	Re-used
Housing and homelessness	Housing and homelessness services provider	Social housing locations, type and uptake Services to people at risk of homelessness	Re-used
Health	Council Population Wellbeing Survey	Life satisfaction Perceived health Social determinants of health	Re-used
	Community health services	Demand for various types of services	Re-used

data-sharing agreements. Datasets were analysed by the researchers in liaison with organisation staff and explored collaboratively through subsequent workshops. These revealed insights, as identified by partner organisations, enabled discussion of caveats of the datasets and included and considered useful ways to present the data while maintaining unidentifiability and paying heed to emergent considerations for partners. For example, we discussed how to present bank data—ultimately this was presented as an index of financial wellbeing, along with other relevant financial wellbeing datasets. The workshop process helped to build relationships, mutual knowledge and trust between the partners, even though most workshops were held online.

Data Analysis

Geospatial visualisation by suburbs was adopted as an analytical approach because most of the datasets had location data, and a place-based approach resonated with partners. As well as considering what open public data was available, each collaborating partner also worked to identify internal datasets that could be re-used and shared. A set of criteria drove identification of datasets to include, as follows:

- data about a topic that aligns with the idea of community resilience;
- data that is analysable by suburb;
- either data subjects that are unidentifiable or data that could be aggregated to achieve non-identifiability;
- caveats around the datasets should be transparent (e.g., the denominator of the dataset, how data was collected and the nature of consent obtained must be known).

Flexibility was required because some datasets were not analysable by suburb, meaning we had to explore other ways to analyse and present some data.

Once each organisation worked through the process of generating a data-sharing agreement, partner organisation managers then shared their dataset(s) with researchers in a suitable format for analysis. Some organisations were able to navigate this stage more quickly than others, depending on data governance practices and availability of dedicated data staff. It was particularly challenging (and for some organisations, impossible) to obtain aggregated data about health services.

Some requested help to export their data. Organising data by suburb was not a standard metric for all organisations. Some collect data at postcode or local government area (LGA) level, which was insufficiently granular for the analyses sought. Suburbs have the disadvantage that they have highly varied population sizes, with some (especially rural localities) having small populations (sometimes <50). This makes it challenging to report results as unidentifiable and reduces the reliability of the Census-derived datasets, because the Australian Bureau of Statistics (ABS) introduces deliberate errors when numbers are low, to protect privacy.

Given the caveats above, datasets were aggregated by suburb where possible and then combined into a single table using the R programming language. The data was exported, joined to a shapefile of suburbs and displayed as a colour-coded geospatial visualisation (map) using PowerBI.

To facilitate comparisons between datasets, data was expressed as proportions of people or households. Different datasets had different samples—so, some were reported as a proportion of the entire population, while others were reported as proportions of other denominators, for example, of respondents to the council survey, by suburb.

Findings

Community Resilience Data Dashboard With most datasets analysed by suburb, the geospatial map format shown in Fig. 2.4 was favoured by most workshop participants. One, two or four maps could be shown on the screen so simultaneous comparisons could be made between different topics or different indicators or datasets about the same broad topic. Ultimately, a data dashboard was generated with an opening interface showing the different topics—Social Connection, Financial Wellbeing and so on. Users could click through to datasets on these topics and view data geospatially visualised as maps with other graphical representations

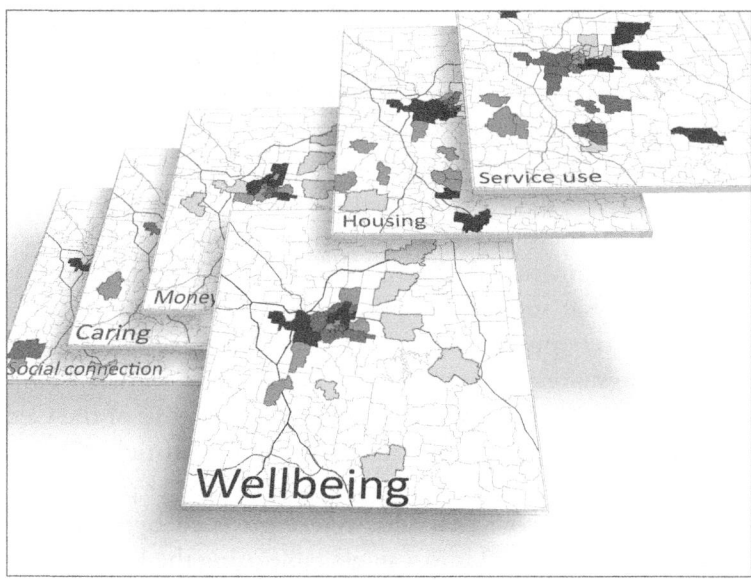

Fig. 2.4 City of Greater Bendigo Community resilience dashboard layers by suburb

also available on-screen for deeper dives. As examples, social connection by suburb also shows a bar graph by age group. Also, suburbs could be clicked on via the map, for more granular information about age group and other demographics, by suburb.

From the Before and After Interviews

Interviews with partner organisations were held at project start and end. Below, issues raised at each stage are summarised, with some example quotes. This serves to highlight the outcomes and process of change for participants.

At the *start of the project*, participants raised three main aspirations: access to data, connecting with data, and building capability. These are summarised below, sometimes with illustrative quotes.

Issues About Data Themes discussed related to lack of access to useful data, including low granularity, insufficiently current data and decline in tailored help from government statistical agencies as their funding has contracted. Partners were frustrated by apparent complete inaccessibility of some datasets (e.g., health data) and hoped the project would help them to find ways to access this data or to find out why it was so hidden. In terms of their own data, partners sometimes noted feeling overwhelmed; for example, "We have just so much data that's in our systems, but actually being able to pull it out and make sense of it and gain insight and intelligence from it is a continuous challenge" (homelessness service). All were intrigued by the potential to use data more and sought to probe the benefits and boundaries of data re-use.

Connecting with Data Participants saw beyond the immediate challenges and thought working together with data could be a catalyst for bringing organisations together for community benefit: "For the health services and other providers as part of the co-op, it might just actually make a difference and be a way we can all collectively advocate for a more interconnected service system. We know at the moment there's a lot of wasted time and effort and money for the service providers, but also the clients who just get shunted from one place to another" (homelessness service).

Building Capability Generating data capability for individuals, organisations and the community was mentioned by most participants: "It's actually growing some capacity in our region to use data together" (women's health service); "So our organisation would have capacity in terms of well, how to design data sets for instance, so that they are analysable" (homelessness service).

By the *end of the project*, partner participants reported feeling more confident and empowered about using data. While they noted insights gained about their community from data analyses, their main reflections were about gains in data capability and collaborative relationships.

Insights About Community Participants noted their preconceptions about more-or-less resilient suburbs were not all borne out when actual datasets were analysed. For one suburb not previously identified as having challenges, data analyses showed consistent deficits, when compared with other suburbs, on multiple resilience indicators. Another suburb perceived as wealthy was suggested—via data analysis—as vulnerable regarding social isolation. Participants noted this made them want to find out more about what was happening in these suburbs, that is, to get some ground-truthing for verification of the information suggested by the data analyses.

Capability Built All participants discussed increases in aspects of data capability. One participant highlighted appreciation of governance matters for using and sharing data, while another had started working with her organisation's data specialist and was working more with data herself. One participant, a data manager at a health organisation, noted the project had made him question his organisation's reluctance to share data: "I've come to question some really tired governance structures. Maybe it's done because we don't understand what's being asked, but really, it's about avoiding the risk. I don't have a solution, but it's become quite obvious" (health service commissioning organisation).

Participants discussed strategies developed to deal with data sharing challenges. For example, making indices to show relative levels of indicators across different suburbs. The power of sophisticated visual displays was highlighted: "I found it really riveting the first time you guys showed those maps… it was just—I loved it" (community health service No. 2); and "Service managers are often quite visually driven, so it's quite powerful in that sense, the power of the data seeing it displayed" (health service commissioning organisation).

Connecting with Data The project helped to build relationships and understanding between organisations. One said: "I guess I've become more aware of the value of the process, perhaps even more so than the value of the outcome" (Council). Talking about and with data was suggested as useful for building knowledge about each other's work through data. Bank participants said they had increased understanding of community challenges and they were able to introduce this knowledge into other discussions within the bank.

Outcomes and Lessons Learned

Overall, the project was well received, with participants more enthused at the end than at the start! Participants worked their way through data challenges as they arose, finding workable solutions. For example, using an index when working with potentially sensitive data to avoid any risk of identifiability. On this topic, participants were primarily concerned about reputational risk for their organisation if someone used analysed data out of context as, in all other respects, they were sure they were re-using data safely and ethically.

Contrary to advice to start with an identified question (The GovLab, 2022), partners in this project benefited from a period of exploring data with each other. At the start, each had their own interests and did not know the work of other organisations. Significantly, they also did not know what data might be forthcoming from their own organisations. The project was a journey of discovery in many ways and, at the end, participants were more knowledgeable and confident to agree next steps of work with data as individual organisations and collaboratively.

While the project started with organisations focused on getting new insights from data, from around half-way through the project, partners agreed a different significant outcome was forthcoming. This was building mutual knowledge through exploring data together that enabled them to see what each could contribute to collective change at community level. Further, they felt empowered to use data in their own work and could see where it might support work of the organisation because they could now understand their operations and services through a lens of data. Some commented they had started to work more confidently on data governance issues. For example, the homelessness service identified gaps in data due to incomplete collection. Managers said they would use new data visualisations to illustrate to staff the benefit of collecting complete datasets.

Data sharing remains problematical. One health organisation simply did not provide data because of perceived challenges of sharing. The data manager explained it was too difficult and time-consuming to navigate the necessary processes—potentially impossible, he thought. Most encouraging was that some managed to navigate data sharing, helping to generate novel analyses that gave new perspectives about the community.

To read more on the City of Greater Bendigo Data Collaborative see Farmer et al. (2022) and https://datacoop.com.au/bendigo/.

Summary

Above we have provided three case studies of data projects from our research and working with partners. While each is different, they all involve collaboration between people and/or organisations with different expertise and perspectives. Similarly, in common, the cases each re-used different datasets and targeted different insights.

Each of the cases provides evidence of learning and changes in relation to using data among staff of the participating organisations. We understand this as *influencing aspects of the data capability* of the organisations that participated. With Case Studies 2 and 3, we were able to evidence changes through *before and after* the project interview data collected. With Case Study 1, the government Business Insights Unit was able to extend its range of types of analyses to inform policy once it learned new techniques of using social media data and found new data sources. In Case Study 2, each organisation's participants expressed surprise that their routine datasets could be repurposed to address real operational and impact measurement challenges. Case Study 3 yielded several examples of changes in awareness, with a participant of one organisation talking about using data much more in her own work and most of the participants remarked on their increasing and more confident interactions with their data staff and teams due to their practical and applied learning from the data collaborative project.

The datasets and analysis techniques varied. While Case Study 1 used innovative Natural Language Processing techniques and public 'big data', linking disparate existing datasets and geospatial analysis was more important for Case Studies 2 and 3. Common to each case was a collaborative process of data discovery, repurposing, linking and *sense-making*. That is, each case shows the significance of identifying and exploring existing datasets and considering how they can be re-used and linked with open and public data. Equally important is the process of data visualisation and, in each case, this enabled processes of collaborative sense-making with the data.

In terms of collaboration, Case Study 1 involved participants from different departments and agencies of government involved in generating, implementing and evaluating policy, but also staff of the Business Insights Unit who were already engaged in aspects of data analysis. In Case Study 2, the participants brought together around projects were from across departments within each of the non-profit organisations. These staff tended to note that they generally work in isolated departmental silos. The data project brought them together to discuss how their work interconnects, driven by working with data. In Case Study 3, the collaboration was among different organisations working in the same community. Interestingly, for each of these different types of collaborations, we noted the same set of emergent phenomena or benefits. Participants got to know and understand each other's work partly through the purposeful action of the process, but also by discussing and probing data generated by the work of different participants at the table (or on the Zoom call). Further, new relationships were forged that could lead to more efficient and effective, and certainly better-informed, future working together. As a participant in Case Study 3 noted, she came to understand "the value of the process even more so than the outcome".

Each case raised barriers and challenges that simultaneously helped to ground participants' expectations about the potential of data analytics, but also sent them back to their organisations to question practices or to make change. For example, in Case Study 3, the homelessness organisation wanted to improve the completeness of its data, and the healthcare commission organisation participant wanted to explore governance practices that served to keep health data hidden. In Case Study 1, participants came to understand the value of aligning the outcomes measurement framework with likely available data from the start, rather than trying to tack things together after policy implementation. All participants came to understand the challenges of sharing data between collaborating partner organisations.

Key Takeaways from This Chapter

In this chapter, we jumped straight into some case studies of non-profits and data analytics. This was done to ensure that readers know what kind of work we are talking about and to illustrate the range of possibilities for types of datasets to work with, visualisations and participants. Key points to take away from this chapter are listed below.

> **Key Takeaways**
>
> - Small, experimental projects that address real-life challenges provide a 'toe in the water' for staff of non-profits and others to test the value that data analytics could have for them.
> - Collaborating on projects led to building relationships across departments and organisations that resulted in better informed data products and to wider understanding among novel networks of people.
> - Work on the projects led to increases in knowledge, awareness and comfort in working with data among participants. We suggest this led to some building of data capability and also to understanding what their organisations need if they are to work more effectively with their data.

Undertaking the case study projects in this chapter with diverse organisational partners led to our conceptualisation of data capability and appreciating the benefits of collaborative working that are explored in Chap. 3.

References

Albury, K., Aryani, A., Farmer, J., Kelly, J., McCosker, A., Silva, S.; Tucker, J., & Woo, J. (2021). *Data for good collaboration: Research report.* Swinburne Social Innovation Research Institute, Swinburne University of Technology. https://doi.org/10.26185/x93d-4v29

Aragon, C., Guha, S., Kogan, M., Muller, M., & Neff, G. (2022). *Human-centered data science: An introduction.* MIT Press.

Australian Bureau of Statistics. (2020a). *1410.0 - Data by region, 2014–19, population and people, ASGS and LGA, 2011, 2014–2019.* Retrieved January 4, 2021, from https://www.abs.gov.au/AUSSTATS/abs@.nsf/DetailsPage/1410.02014-19?OpenDocument

Australian Bureau of Statistics. (2020b). *2071.0.55.001 – Census of population and housing: Commuting to work.* Retrieved January 4, 2021, from https://www.abs.gov.au/ausstats/abs@.nsf/mf/2071.0.55.001

City of Melbourne. (2020). *Transport strategy 2030.* Retrieved January 4, 2021, from https://www.melbourne.vic.gov.au/SiteCollectionDocuments/transport-strategy-2030-city-of-melbourne.pdf

Farmer, J., Aryani, A., Tucker, J., & Woo, J. (2022). *City of Greater Bendigo data co-op: A place-based data collaboration focused on community resilience.* Swinburne Social Innovation Research Institute. https://doi.org/10.25916/psea-0856

Government of Victoria. (2020). *A framework for place-based approaches.* Retrieved April 7, 2022, from https://www.vic.gov.au/framework-place-based-approaches

McCosker, A., Farmer, J., & Soltani Panah, A. (2020). *Community responses to family violence: Charting policy outcomes using novel data sources, text mining and topic modelling.* Swinburne University of Technology. Retrieved April 7, 2022, from https://apo.org.au/node/278041

Murray, B., Falkenberger, E., & Saxena, P. (2015). *Data walks: An innovative way to share data with communities.* Urban Institute. Retrieved April 4, 2022, from https://www.urban.org/research/publication/data-walks-innovative-way-share-data-communities

Payton Scally, C., Burnstein, E., & Gerken, M. (2020). *In search of 'good' rural data: Measuring rural prosperity.* Urban Institute, Aspen Institute Community Strategies Group. Retrieved April 7, 2022, from https://www.urban.org/research/publication/search-good-rural-data

State Government of Victoria. (n.d.). *Family violence outcomes framework*. Retrieved April 8, 2022, from https://www.vic.gov.au/family-violence-outcomes-framework

The GovLab. (2022). *Data Collaboratives: Creating public value by exchanging data*. Retrieved January 5, 2021, from https://www.thegovlab.org/project/project-datacollaboratives-org

Open Access This chapter is licensed under the terms of the Creative Commons Attribution 4.0 International License (http://creativecommons.org/licenses/by/4.0/), which permits use, sharing, adaptation, distribution and reproduction in any medium or format, as long as you give appropriate credit to the original author(s) and the source, provide a link to the Creative Commons licence and indicate if changes were made.

The images or other third party material in this chapter are included in the chapter's Creative Commons licence, unless indicated otherwise in a credit line to the material. If material is not included in the chapter's Creative Commons licence and your intended use is not permitted by statutory regulation or exceeds the permitted use, you will need to obtain permission directly from the copyright holder.

3

Data Capability Through Collaborative Data Action

In Chap. 2, we presented case studies of some of our data projects that involved working with non-profits and other types of organisations and re-using varied datasets. Each of these projects saw participants move from curiosity about data analytics, to a growth in confidence around using terminology, understanding techniques and having a grasp of non-profits' internal data resources. We argue that this represents the participants making progress in building aspects of the data capability of their organisations as well as understanding gaps. From our experience, successful results happen in data projects when people with diverse backgrounds and perspectives collaborate to explore issues of direct relevance to them, drawing on varied expertise, infrastructure and datasets. Organisations have existing data practices and resources, and so experimenting together with novel analytical techniques and types of datasets can help partners with a social mission to understand what to do next to extend and tailor their future data practices.

What we found through our projects with non-profits, then, is that *collaborative data action* supports the *building of data capability*. As depicted in our case studies, collaborations can draw across teams within a single organisation, across a set of like-minded organisation partners

© The Author(s) 2023
J. Farmer et al., *Data for Social Good*, https://doi.org/10.1007/978-981-19-5554-9_3

and externally with researcher partners and others. In this chapter, we move from examples showing the sometimes messy business of non-profits working with novel datasets, to attempting to secure some concepts and processes that underpin non-profits working with data analytics. Thus, we explore here what we think data capability looks like for non-profits and provide our methodology for supporting capability to build through collaborative data action. In doing so, we suggest priority topics for non-profits to address, principally around establishing responsible data governance and being clear about ethics and consent.

Again, we note this is based on our practical work up to 2022, and from our base in Australia. Law and practices relevant to non-profit data analytics will be different in other countries and regions and are changing over time.

Understanding Data Capability

Drawing on our own research, we suggest that at an organisational level, *data capability* is a holistic resource. It involves having in place the interconnected aspects of appropriate *staff roles and skills, technologies,* and *data management practices and processes* to fulfil what an organisation needs and wants to do with data. In data science, *capability* has a dual meaning, relating both to human competencies and technical components like software, hardware and database systems. In our work, we retain this sense of data capability as multi-faceted and interconnected with multiple technical and human attributes. Data capability is additionally hard to pin down, we suggest, because it is situated or adaptive to context—that is, data capability will vary according with each non-profit's work, mission and vision in their operating context. We realise this can make data capability seem elusive and hard to measure, but we suggest it is most realistic to think of it as this combined, evolving, overall resource.

Data capability is related to data management and data governance. *Data management* is about having a system of internal practices and mechanisms for controlling data within an organisation. DAMA International describe centralised, distributed and hybrid models of data management, referring to the way parts of an organisation can work collectively and independently when managing and working with data (2017, p. 565). *Data governance* is the framework of ethics, safety and accountability practices that interweaves with and shapes how data management is done. We return to explore data governance as a foundation for data capability later in this chapter.

We suggest *data capability* is the *outcome* that non-profits should be aspiring to achieve as they increasingly use data analytics. However, it is not static, rather it is refreshed and continually reformed via *processes* of engaging with datasets and new ways of working with, and using, data. This means the data capability of an organisation formulates through adaptation and change via ongoing experimenting and learning with data. Considering our Chap. 2 case study projects as processes of learning, participants were generally more knowledgeable, confident and comfortable with using data and interpreting data analyses by the end of projects. While we did not have formal evaluation in all our projects, we witnessed instances of increased engagement with data among a wide range of staff members (not just data or IT professionals) and the adoption of more sophisticated data practices, often across teams and individuals who didn't normally work together. Participants developed agility and confidence in their ability to determine when and which types of data analytics and visualisations would be useful (or not) in specific contexts. They were generally more excited and animated about the potential of working with data into the future. Underpinning these findings, participants also talked about changes that would need to be made, particularly to their data management and data governance practices. Examples of this include questioning risk aversion in sharing datasets and talking about the need for strategic consideration of reconfiguring data governance. These are all aspects indicating the way data capability forms and provide examples of the multiple and small steps by which data capability develops in relation to context.

In our projects, we saw non-profits' data capability influenced through processes of practising with using their *own* internal datasets for insights about *their* problems and challenges. This seemed impactful, compared with participating in generic training modules or engaging with generic resource kits (as we tried in Case 2 described in Chap. 2). While building data capability still implies financial investment in technologies, infrastructures and skilled people, collaborative practice can help participants work out what their organisation needs and target their spending on priorities. Depending on who is involved in collaborative projects, progress in data capability can be activated strategically (from the top down) where senior managers participate, or from the ground up, through the action of practitioners in consumer and client-facing roles.

Responding to sectoral interest in increasing data analytics expertise across the non-profit sector, several frameworks have emerged for measuring and monitoring development of organisational resources related to having data capability (for example, see the work of https://data.org in the US). Some stakeholders—such as philanthropic foundations or non-profit representative bodies—seek to benchmark how individual non-profits compare in their *data maturity* against others in the sector. They also apply frameworks to identify sectoral strengths and gaps. Some assessment tools have rating scales, for example, with a low score for initial or ad hoc practices, to a higher score for systematically *managed* or *optimised* data practices (see, e.g., DAMA International's rating scale [DAMA International, 2017, p. 531]). In the UK, Data Orchard's *Framework for Measuring Data Maturity* in non-profit organisations (Data Orchard, 2019) aims for expert-level resources and practices or *mastery* as the goal, with maturity examined on dimensions including data uses, analysis, leadership, culture, tools and skills. We explored the difference we see between data capability and data maturity or data literacy in Chap. 1, saying why we prefer the idea of data capability as a goal for non-profits. This is mainly because we do not think data resources like human skills, technologies and practices should be fixed, but rather adaptive relative to each non-profit's context, strategy, mission, size and so on.

While we express reservations with static frameworks, one of our own collaborative research projects driven by perspectives from multiple Australian non-profits led to the creation of a broad data capability framework (Yao et al., 2021). This identifies attributes participating non-profits considered central to their data work. These are assigned to four domains: (1) *access* to quality data; (2) data *skills* and ability; (3) effective *technology* systems, tools and data infrastructure; and (4) responsible data *governance* (see Yao et al., 2021). However, even given this framework, we have found more generally in our work with non-profits that rather than embracing levels of attainment on a fixed scale, many emphasise they have nuanced and varying needs and goals for data use. Consequently, the value of frameworks, for them, was suggested as offering shorthand checklists against which to reflect on organisational strengths and gaps against an indicative industry standard.

Building the more holistic resource of data capability also enables non-profits to influence and activate beyond their own operational matters. For larger organisations, this could involve sharing data expertise with other, smaller organisations and helping to develop sector-wide collective responses to social problems. Alternatively, it could involve developing shared data resources or data collaboratives like the *Humanitarian Data Exchange (HDX)* (https://data.humdata.org/). Having data capability provides a foundation for a non-profit to partner with their clients and communities on data projects with wide social benefit. Hendey et al. (2020) depict this as non-profits contributing to a wider social mission of enabling *community data capability*. While no single model of community data capability exists, the authors argue that when data capability and resources are democratised and available to those who can benefit, "communities will be better equipped to partner with foundations, apply data to understand issues, and take the actions needed to achieve the ambitious outcomes that [philanthropic] foundations seek" (Hendey et al., 2020, p. 1). Non-profits are well placed, due to their work and missions, to drive community data capability goals.

A Collaborative Data Action Methodology

Our case studies in Chap. 2 show where we have worked in collaborations with non-profits, sometimes with staff members across teams of one organisation and sometimes across organisations. In those projects, we observed teams and groups addressing a data challenge, but also in the process, developing or at least influencing their data capability. Some of the impacts of working collaboratively are highlighted at the end of Chap. 2. Observing the projects, their direct outcomes and wider impressive impacts has made us committed to collaborative working; and in this section, we talk specifically about our collaborative data action methodology.

There could be a range of different ways that non-profits could gain data capability through collaborative working. This could be through working with other non-profits with large or specialist data science teams, working more effectively across teams within their own organisations, or accessing data collaboratives or external *data for social good* initiatives (see this book's appendix). The point is to engage with others with a shared social mission and to gather a team of people that combines useful knowledge, skills and perspectives.

There are some very practical implications of collaborating that we have already alluded to. These include accessing others' expertise and resources to help improve your own organisation's access to costly resources and to learn what you need by efficient contextualised learning. There are also wider benefits of collaborating. Firstly, the field of data analytics is moving so fast at present that it requires dedicated specialists to keep up. This is just data science, of course, and the fields of social justice and addressing a social mission have also changed dramatically in response to the pandemic and its ongoing effects. A simple benefit of collaborating is that it gives access to a wider range of human resources to keep up with changes in knowledge and techniques across fields of expertise and practice. Collaborating is also a way to help keep small, potentially niche non-profits operating as the sector becomes more corporate and favours larger organisations. Finally, and importantly, organisations collaborating with data for social good help to build the field. Working together generates new networks, social capital and communities of practice between organisations that will impact more widely to foster community data capability.

In our projects, we use a process of collective 'learning by doing' or *collaborative data action*. The process allows for experimentation and adaptation. It allows individuals within non-profits, including senior managers and board members, to see how working with data can help to integrate their operations and services across departments (i.e., wider benefits). And it can help to empower and activate grass-roots practitioners in incorporating data work as part of their daily practice.

While data projects will vary in their precise process due to different participants, questions, data and timelines, we have found there are a consistent set of main activities that punctuate collaborative data action in our data projects with non-profits. Figure 3.1 outlines these main activities, giving an approximate chronology.

At this point, we highlight that we have mainly used the collaborative data action methodology when working with organisations seeking to find out whether data analytics is useful for them. This could suggest it works best for those setting out from *a low base*; however, that is not the whole story. For example, the bank in Case Study 3 had a large and sophisticated data analytics team, and in Case Study 1, we worked with the business insights unit of government, a team specialised in data analytics to inform policy. Rather, then, perhaps the collaborative data action methodology is best regarded as a mechanism for experimenting with data analytics. Experimenting can involve starting out, but it can also involve trialling different techniques for data analysis or addressing

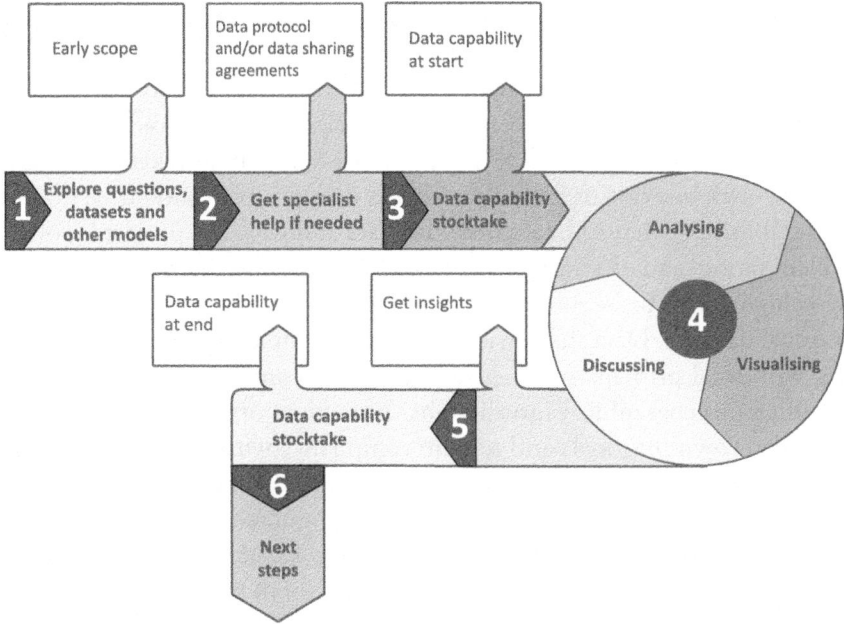

Fig. 3.1 Process of collaborative data action for non-profits' data projects

more ambitious goals. Thus, collaborative data action can involve organisations that are skilled-up and advanced in working with data. Of course, a key element here is that an organisation can access a range of knowledge, technology or other resources that can help to work with data in different ways or inject other types of knowledge (e.g., from social science or community practice) into data analytics.

In our projects, we tried out various activities as part of processes of experimenting and collaborating in data projects. Some approaches we initially included turned out to be blind alleys—for example, the general educational webinars we provided in Case Study 2 turned out to be less well-received than learning by doing experienced with participants in addressing their organisations' challenges and using their data. Ultimately, we arrived at a methodology comprising a relatively consistent set of activities that helped to produce project outputs and processes and within which participants said they experienced learning and enjoyment.

Steps in our collaborative data action methodology involve different kinds of actions (see Table 3.1). Some steps involve *exploring*. Step 1, for example, is about simultaneously exploring ideas from previous case studies, questions to focus on, and useful datasets all in order to test the feasibility of undertaking a data project and deciding its initial scope.

Step 2 involves turning to specialist experts examples, and precedent for help to formally get started. If a project is being undertaken internally and involves just one organisation, then a data protocol should be drawn up establishing what is to be done with data and why. If a project involves collaborating and sharing data across organisations, then data sharing agreements will be required that allow partners to work together with internal datasets. Data sharing is notoriously complex and requires engaging with legal principles influenced by the laws and guidance that apply in different geographical jurisdictions. Individual organisations will also have their own protocols and require compliance with sectoral guidance. We have indicated some current resources that can help to think about data sharing and what is required in data sharing agreements in the appendix. Data sharing across organisations is also revisited later in this chapter.

In our projects we also found that it was useful to build in some formal *stocktake* or evaluation 'before and after' opportunities to facilitate reflection at the start and end of data projects. This enables participants

Table 3.1 Steps in the process of collaborative data action for non-profits' data projects

Step	Actions	Goal/achievement
Early steps		
1. EXPLORE initial question or focus, potential data sources and similar data projects	Consider what topics or questions the data project might target and what internal and open datasets there might be that could address the question. Explore examples of other data projects and their output visualisations and engage with potential data collaborators with a shared interest and useful skills	Draft early scope of a project, including questions, datasets and collaborators across teams and/or other organisations
2. Bring in SPECIALIST HELP for establishing data protocols or agreements	Work with a legal team and data collaborators to establish data protocols and, if needed, data sharing agreements matching jurisdiction/sector legal requirements	Have agreed data protocol and/or data sharing agreements
3. Pre-project data capability STOCKTAKE	Conduct an early 'stocktake' to establish all participants' goals, data challenges and gaps in capability	Summary of data capability at the start
Doing the project		
4. ITERATE through cycles of analysing & visualising datasets, using DATA WALKS to EXPLORE and then analysing other datasets and/or ADAPTING visualisations and questions	Begin initial data analysis using identified data sources and generate visualisations to discuss findings as a group. Then repeat this process until a focused question has been addressed or insights gained, that is, until the group is sufficiently satisfied they have attained their goals in the data project	Identify insights and visualisations to address focus questions
End of project		
5. End of project data capability STOCKTAKE	Conduct follow-up stocktake to find out what has changed, any learning and remaining gaps	Summary of changes in data capability
6. NEXT STEPS	Think about what has been learned and what should be done next	Acknowledge outcomes of the data project and agree next steps

to identify changes in their attitudes and practices at individual and organisational levels. This stocktake can be simple and involve thinking about and documenting concerns about data, aspirations for using data and assessments of expertise and readiness. At the end of projects, it can be about what was learned and what remain gaps. Stocktakes are at steps 3 and 5 of our methodology. We did not include formal data gathering stocktakes in our early projects (e.g., Case Study 1), but we discovered its value in Case Study 2 and then applied this learning in Case Study 3 and other projects since.

Step 4 involves *iteration* of several activities of working with datasets, aiming to answer questions and point to next steps. It involves analysing and visualising data and then exploring and discussing results. Once analyses and visualisations have been explored, it is usually necessary to cycle back a few times to identify other useful datasets and analyse and visualise these—all with the target of getting closer to an 'answer' to questions set or topics to be explored via the data analyses and to find out more about the topic(s) involved in exploring a question.

In our projects we employed cycles of workshops using an approach inspired by the data walks method of the Urban Institute's National Neighborhood Indicators Partnerships (Murray et al., 2015). Data walks involve workshop discussion where participants are shown visualised analyses, and encouraged to ask questions, engage with what *they see* in the data and sense-check this given their grass-roots knowledge. Iterative rounds of data analysis followed by discussion help participants to make sense of data that has been analysed and visualised and to discuss with each other, the stories they perceive to be told in the data. Visualisations are an important part of data walks, as diagrams, geospatial maps and graphs tend to be commonly accessible to participants from different backgrounds. In our projects, data walks were useful for considering topic-based insights but also for stimulating technical queries about datasets and exploring issues about data collection affecting interpretation of analyses.

Based on feedback on analysed and visualised data from the workshops, new datasets may be identified and analysed, new types of analysis might be conducted with the same datasets or different visualisation techniques might be employed. Then new analyses and visualisations would be brought back for further discussion and sense-making at a workshop, with the idea being to cycle through multiple workshops until a question or focus topic has been sufficiently addressed. Open-ended cycles of iteration can be challenging to explain in funding applications and contracts, so it may be useful to consider that in our projects we found three to four iterative cycles generally produced useful findings. After more than three to four cycles, the project might lose impetus and participants might lose interest.

Exploring questions and datasets collaboratively in workshops helps to generate a shared understanding and language around data use and outcomes sought. The collaborative methodology ensures that each participant shares their perspective in these sessions and their take on featured questions and data. This means that no single department within an organisation or dominant partner, if working across organisations, imposes their viewpoint. Taking an exploratory approach can generate wider buy-in by showing that different participants can have different, equally valid, ways of understanding a question, problem or challenge being addressed. Understanding can be gained here about how problems are multi-faceted, prompted by discussing insights suggested by data analyses.

This working between question(s) and dataset(s) that we describe involves processes of *adaptation*, with a goal of matching data with questions. Sometimes the adaptive process leads to framing a question in a different way. At other times, there is a realisation that a whole and perfect dataset to answer a pre-defined question does not exist, prompting a turn to other data that can *inform* about a question if not answer it directly. An example here was where the state government participants in Case Study 1 came to realise that a comprehensive dataset precisely aligning with changed attitudes to family violence did not exist. Instead, we harnessed Twitter data and news media data with textual data analytics to show a quite granular change in topics discussed over time. At the same time, we know there are caveats about some of these datasets. For example, Twitter users are a self-selecting, more policy-aware community. The government itself periodically conducts a Community Attitudes Survey covering attitudes to family violence but, again, responses in that dataset are from self-selected participants who tend to be older and more educated. Together, the data from the three sources (Twitter, news media, community survey) can be *triangulated* to give richer, though still not comprehensive, information about the extent of discussion (in this case related to family violence), variety of topics discussed and responses to different types of policy and other events.

The adaptive way of working between topics and questions that we adopt is one way that our approach is potentially distinct. Other data project methodologies we have seen emphasise pursuing and identifying *a precise problem or question* before proceeding to data analysis (e.g., The GovLab, n.d.). While it is important to have a broad initial focus, we have found it can be difficult for non-profit partners to identify specific questions or *pain points* at the start of a data project. This can be because participants don't have a grasp of what data might be available, what might be possible (and not possible) with data analytics and may need time to understand the work of other participants. In our experience, focus for projects does happen, but it emerges or sharpens through working with data and discussing questions iteratively and learning what is possible and useful. Being open as to focus can be challenging for non-profits to justify in funding applications, so a useful strategy is to identify a broad topic to explore from the start.

Following the end of project stocktake at step 5, the conclusion of the process is to acknowledge what has been achieved in terms of data product outputs and wider outcomes in relation to learning or partnerships and to decide what next steps are appropriate, if any.

Finding Your Data Collaborators

In this book, we propose that building data capability should not be a solo practice. Building data capability could be done through working on experimental data projects and these might benefit, depending on their scope and goals, from the skills and perspectives of a range of different people, teams and organisations. Preferably, this would also include lived experience consumers, clients and citizens because they will help to make more insightful, ethical data products and extend data capability within the community. In Chap. 2, we showed that the collaborations we have worked within took multiple forms. They involved working across departments *inside* an organisation (as with Good Cycles and Yooralla in

Case Study 2, and multiple departments and agencies of government in Case Study 1) and working *across* non-profits and other community organisations (as in the City of Greater Bendigo data collaborative project in Case Study 3). In each case, our university-based social data analytics team brought expertise in data science and social science, as well as access to technologies and safe, secure practices. The collaborating partners brought their expertise which also involved data analytics skills and understanding of problems and contexts. When we were re-using non-profits' internal datasets, their staff could inform about how data was collected and what was included and excluded in datasets.

We term the various participants—people, teams, organisations—in data projects as data collaborators. While a range of perspectives makes the collaboration more than the sum of its parts, clearly the main thing we are focused on is the potential offered by injecting advanced know-how about data science and analytics. It is a premise of this book that the projects we describe are about building (greater) data capability for non-profits. In our projects, the university team brought access to advanced data science knowledge, technology and practices. While here we mainly focus on university teams, there is a range of ways to access collaborating partners with data science expertise. Non-profits might partner with other, perhaps larger, non-profits that have specialist data analytics teams or collaborate together to approach some external entity with expertise. In the appendix, we suggest some data analytics initiatives that have a particular mission to build data analytics capability of the non-profit sector. Initiatives working to support data capability development are sometimes termed *data intermediaries* or *data institutions* (Hardinges & Keller, 2022). These might offer opportunities for mentoring and learning in partnerships (Perkmann & Schildt, 2014; Susha et al., 2017), although some data intermediaries are more engaged as *brokers* between organisations and data owners (Sangwan, 2021). In encouraging collaborations between non-profits and other social sector actors to grow data capability and community data capability, we align with the concept of the organisational partners envisaged in the National Neighborhood Indicators Partnerships. Many of those partnerships combine local community organisations, non-profits and councils working with university social data analytics labs (Arena & Hendey, 2019).

As university researchers ourselves, we recognise and suggest the potential of seeking out a university social data analytics lab to work with. The opportunity is that such labs will often share the social mission orientation of non-profits, and there are many examples of labs situated in universities around the world. Some university data analytics labs will be actively looking to partner for access to 'real-life' projects for training data science students. As one example, the Center for Urban and Regional Affairs (CURA) at the University of Minnesota (https://www.cura.umn.edu) links academics and students with community organisations to generate data analytics projects, specialising in data for neighbourhood planning. Other examples of university data labs working with non-profits can be found in the literature; for example, Tripp et al. (2020) describe a partnership between an education and literacy non-profit and the West Georgia University's Data and Visualisation Lab. Of course, generally universities do still require funding to work on data projects. This could come directly from a non-profit or partnerships could be formed with university labs to apply, together, for funding.

Different partners collaborating with data and sharing knowledge and skills generates new *boundary spaces* (Susha et al., 2017). These enable novel combined skillsets to emerge, helping to grow a future workforce of people that understand both non-profit work and data analytics. Research literature describing *how to do* data analytics for social good emphasises the significance of a diverse team, including data scientists, social scientists, practitioners and lived experience consumers and clients (e.g., Williams, 2020).

Responsible Data Governance

In the last part of this chapter, we focus on practices that all non-profits will already have considered in some way if they are working with data: these are practices of data governance. Data governance is understood here as having the systems and processes so that an organisation can ensure data is managed and analysed responsibly, legally and ethically. It involves having clear mechanisms through which an organisation, and its people, are held to account about the production and use of data. We focus on data governance here because it is a priority consideration for an organisation working to re-use its data. Having appropriate data governance in place is a necessary precursor to working in data projects, particularly when engaging with other organisations in a collaboration. It is also a feature that organisations can start working on without having to wait to find data collaborators to work with.

Having responsible data governance enables an organisation to have safe and secure data, accountability, quality assurance and ethical data practice. Active engagement across organisations in data governance will result in a positive data culture, with all staff, clients, consumers, managers and board members engaged in well-considered, ethical data work.

Co-ordinated practices of responsible data governance should be thought through and implemented by any organisation collecting and using data. Data governance sits around, permeates and directs data management, including affecting who works with data (roles and skills), technologies and how they are used, and the nature of practices and processes in handling, storing and analysing data. Governance will need to be able to respond to changing organisation requirements to use different datasets with different types of analyses. Data governance needs to be integral to organisational governance, not seen as separate, as it relates to whole of organisation best practice and accountability. With increased production, storage and use of data, and the consequent potential for many forms of data harm, data governance has become an important aspect of organisational governance (Redden et al., 2020). This includes aligning and interweaving data practices with the protocols and policies that guide an organisation's practices around ethics, risk management, compliance, administration and privacy (Governance Institute of Australia, 2022).

The significance of data governance makes it a strategic organisational issue, and the priority data governance is given by organisations will determine what they can do with data. The values inherent in how data governance is implemented shapes the goals and outcomes of using data. This includes ways of viewing relationships—customers and clients can be 'mined', and their data 'extracted', or they can be consenting collaborators, with their needs aligned to how data is used.

Depictions of data governance in the research literature can suggest a commercial emphasis inappropriate for the non-profit sector. For example, Otto (2011, p. 47) defines data governance as "a companywide framework for assigning decision-related rights and duties in order to be able to adequately handle data as a company asset" (cited in Alhassan et al., 2018, p. 301). Objectifying data in this way, as a kind of commodity, serves to disregard the integrative relationship between data, people and services. It might be said, therefore, that non-profit data governance models compare, but also differ, in ways from those of commercial organisations, with differences driven by mission, context and vision of each non-profit.

While frameworks for data governance tend to be internally focused, the requirement for formal policies and protocols is increasingly driven by interactions with the external environment. This is especially true in relation to embarking on data collaborations involving other organisations and sharing datasets (Verhulst, 2021). Indeed, increasingly, experts advocate for data stewards as a kind of data governance role for organisations serious about developing data capability (Verhulst et al., 2020). "Data stewardship is a concept with deep roots in the science and practice of data collection, sharing, and analysis. Reflecting the values of fair information practice, data stewardship denotes an approach to the management of data, particularly data that can identify individuals" (Rosenbaum, 2010, p. 1442). Data stewards would be responsible for understanding the datasets that exist in organisations and ensuring their quality. One role for organisational data stewards would be in bringing internal datasets into collaborations across organisations to facilitate data collaboratives and data sharing.

While designating a data steward signifies organisational acknowledgement that data governance is important and demands an owner, the holistic nature of data governance suggests it as also collective action issue. As touched on in Chap. 1, clients, customers and other people in the data of non-profits and involved in its collection, should be included in designing data governance that assures fairness and empowerment. Some researchers have demonstrated "the value in theorizing data governance as a collective action problem and argue for the necessity of ensuring researchers and practitioners achieve a common understanding of the inherent challenges, as a first step towards developing data governance solutions that are viable in practice" (Benfeldt et al., 2020, p. 299).

Topics at the heart of responsible data governance are ethics and consent and are featured below. Clarity about ethics and relationships of consent and trust is essential because of the imperative of accountability to all of the people who are stakeholders in the data. Getting ethics and consent right sets non-profits up to achieve in more ambitious, innovative and strategic efforts of working with data beyond basic use of internal datasets—that is, looking to data collaboratives and data sharing.

Data culture is closely related to data governance. When data governance is working well, it becomes embedded and part of the everyday practice of organisations, contributing to a positive data culture. Clearly data culture can be of varying quality, dependent on attributes such as inclusion in governance, ethics-orientation and embeddedness in roles, operations and strategy. We understand data culture here as the organisationally embedded ways of understanding and working with data ethically and safely. Central to having a positive data culture is instilling and embedding genuine concern about the relationship between the people who generate the data (bearing in mind Williams' assertion that "data are people" [Williams, 2020, p. 220]) and what can thus be done with data. Disciplined thinking about consent and trust must be established and maintained. Data culture relates to the values of organisations around enabling and empowering people (staff, clients, customers and others) and accountability to these stakeholders. While we found little written about organisational data culture and its development, it seems an issue that is close to consideration of organisational ethics.

Data Ethics and Consent

Issues of ethics and consent are fundamental to consider from the start of any data collection. They are difficult to 'retrofit' if a non-profit decides it wants to re-use data originally collected to measure outputs or for statutory reporting. Clearly as well, addressing these issues is not about organising so that a non-profit can have the data it wants to work with. The question of who owns the data, and is *in* the data, is the ethical issue here. As highlighted in Chap. 1, work is ongoing internationally to partner with people who are (in) data to drive its ethical collection and use. Indigenous scholars have perhaps gone furthest in showing why and how marginalised groups should be driving collection and use of data about them. For example, Kukutai and Taylor (2016) documented the importance of affirming Indigenous people's rights to self-determination via recognition of data sovereignty.

Some practical guidance and resources to help non-profits achieve ethical data use and re-use have been developed by data initiatives internationally (e.g., National Neighborhood Indicators Partnership, 2018; NESTA, 2022; and see the appendix). In our own work in collaborations with non-profits, we have found that some materials about ethics and consent can be high-level, too general or too specific in their nature for application across diverse contexts. As a body of advice, the sheer amount of guidance can even seem overwhelming. Perhaps because of this, among the communities of data practice where we have participated, non-profits tend to share and adapt data management, privacy and security policies among their networks and to develop norms around data collection and use through cumulative processes. Data ethics is not always explicitly discussed, even if care and responsibility is taken in all data practices. Here, we suggest how to begin to think about and apply data ethics, irrespective of precise frameworks or protocols, by focusing on establishing relationships of care and consent in data production and use.

Firstly, there are legal considerations in using personal data and data governance is entwined with regulation and increasingly the subject of law reform across different global jurisdictions. Laws governing personal data have dealt mainly with issues of privacy and cybersecurity but are becoming more complicated as technology develops and services become 'digital-first'. Because these are jurisdiction-specific, all we can suggest here is to consult jurisdictional sector representative bodies and the government agencies established to guide and inform adherence to relevant laws. If working with *sensitive data*—for example, personal data, especially where it concerns health, race, sexuality, beliefs and associations—data ethics and data management practices (like secure or encrypted storage, de-identification and access protocols) are high priority. Non-profits should consider working with a legal advisor with relevant understanding of data, information and privacy regulation.

Beyond compliance with relevant data regulation, there is growing recognition of the need to begin with ethical frameworks and develop policies and practices for data use that involve carefully established trust and consent. By consent we do not simply mean the kinds of contractual agreement documents or pages that people sign or click 'OK' to engage with a service. These are instruments for establishing consent, but we are referring more broadly to the relationships developed within an organisation and with customers, clients and citizens around data collection and use.

Gaining consent for data use is a *process* for ensuring good data practices and relationships. It does not happen just once but is maintained and re-established as part of managing client and customer relationships and ensuring informed agreement with any new use of data. This is often approached through the establishment of norms (based on an organisations' values) of what an organisation *should* do to work safely with personal data, and with *care*. Two useful guiding principles are that any data collected should be necessary, and the purpose should be transparent and communicated clearly to those involved in generating the data or to whom it refers. This requires deciding what data is to be collected and its purpose, and an organisation may have detailed policy documents and ethical frameworks to help guide those decisions. As raised in Chap. 1, non-profits should be working towards involving consumers or clients (i.e., often the subjects in and of non-profits internal datasets), in codesigning these practices, avoiding tokenistic forms of inclusion.

As part of data governance, a comprehensive set of data ethics protocols and policies can help to drive a positive organisational data culture. With data collection increasing, data ethics scholars have identified core concerns to be addressed. Mittelstadt and Floridi (2016) emphasise informed consent, privacy (including data anonymisation and data protection), ownership and control over data, epistemology and objectivity (or data quality), and data-driven inequality "between those who have or lack the necessary resources to analyse increasingly large datasets" (Mittelstadt & Floridi, 2016, p. 303). Franzke et al. (2021) describe the development of a Data Ethics Decision Aid (DEDA), used to reflect on and guide decisions about data projects in the governmental context. The Open Data Institute's (2019) Data Ethics Canvas identifies 14 categories to help assess ethical aspects of using data in an organisational or government context.

There are increasing moves for organisations to collaborate to share reused data generated through their work. Our City of Greater Bendigo data collaborative (see Case Study 3 in Chap. 2), for example, was developed because seven community organisations wanted to find out whether pooling their data could help to generate new insights about community resilience. There are important ethical dimensions to such data re-use in the context of data sharing. There are logistical aspects to data sharing—why do it, what data and for what kinds of analysis? But data sharing and re-use are underpinned by governance and ethical issues first, because data use is contingent on the arrangements in place to ensure data is treated ethically, safely and with care. Foremost is clarity about whether consent for different types of use has been established or needs to be (re-)established with those who are the subjects of the data. Consent might have been established for a primary purpose but not for a secondary purpose. In Europe, the General Data Protection Regulation (GDPR) laws restrict data re-use and suggest re-establishing consent for secondary use (European Parliament and the Council of the European Union, 2016). In that jurisdiction, data can be re-used for a secondary purpose if its use relates to the primary purpose and a person would reasonably expect it to be used for the secondary purpose. For health information or other sensitive information, re-use is contingent on a direct link with the primary purpose for data collection.

Ensuring that ethics and consent issues are well considered, clear and codified, and comply with jurisdictional data legislation and practice is significant to guiding a non-profit's internal use of data. This becomes crucial when starting to work with other organisations to re-use data in collaborations. Ethics and consent practice govern the extent to which analyses of a non-profit's internal data can be undertaken, shown or shared with other organisations. While this might sound straightforward, consider what is potentially hidden in that deceptively simple idea of showing or sharing. In our City of Greater Bendigo Case Study 3 (see Chap. 2), it was one thing to look at each organisations' visualised data analyses in a workshop of seven organisations' representatives, but we then had to work out whether the visualisations could be seen by other staff or even explored in wider community engagement exercises. If visualised analyses of data could be shared, then in what formats? For example, ultimately percentages at suburb level were converted into an index of high to low relative quantities (e.g., in relation to wealth or demand for types of services) in our visualisations. This meant these could be shared beyond immediate workshop participants. This decision was taken on the basis of adhering to consents given/obtained for each dataset. The decision also responded to perceived potential reputational risks where community members might react adversely to seeing visualisations of datasets, for example, bank or service demand data, even if completely unidentifiable to individuals or households.

Data Sharing for Collective Gain

Given the issues just raised about data sharing in the example of Case Study 3, finally in this chapter we focus specifically on the data governance issue of consent and secondary use of datasets and data sharing. Because an organisation might want to move beyond re-using their own internal data and collaborate with others around data, obtaining appropriate consent is fundamental to data collection. A broad framework of thinking that we have used to guide our projects is the *Five Safes* model, initially developed by the UK Data Service (2017) to enable researchers to access government and sensitive data. This model was later adopted by the Australian Office of the National Data Commissioner as principles for access to and re-use of public sector data while maintaining data privacy and security. Though developed for public data sharing, the principles of the Five Safes are equally applicable as a guide to safe data sharing in the non-profit sector. It helps as a high-level framework to evaluate major risk areas and to identify steps to minimise the risk of data re-use. The Five Safes model draws attention to issues of sharing data in the domains of:

- Projects: ensuring data is shared for an appropriate purpose that delivers a public benefit.
- People: ensuring those using the data have the appropriate authority to access it.
- Settings: ensuring the environment in which the data is shared minimises the risk of unauthorised use or disclosure.
- Data: ensuring appropriate and proportionate protections are applied to the data.
- Output: ensuring output from the data-sharing arrangement is appropriately safeguarded before any further sharing or release.

Data collaboratives have become more widely discussed, as organisations recognise the value of working together to address community challenges. In our case studies, we showed an example of a community data collaborative where a range of organisations united around their internal datasets to explore for insights about community resilience. Our data collaborative projects use our Data Co-op platform (https://datacoop.com.au) that has software, hardware, management practices, multi-disciplinary skills and data governance to support safe data sharing. Funded to the tune of over AU$1,000,000 by the Australian Research Council and five universities, this scale of investment in data collaborative infrastructure is outside the scope of most non-profits. We propose this supports our suggestions above that non-profits seeking to develop more ambitious data analytics projects could usefully collaborate to achieve more ambitious and complex projects.

Data collaborations can have various forms and work together for different reasons (Susha et al., 2017). Verhulst and Sangokoya (2015) give an example of humanitarian organisations working to share data for disaster relief. NCEL, Nepal's largest mobile operator, shared anonymised mobile phone data with the non-profit Swedish organisation Flowminder. With this data, Flowminder mapped where and how people moved in the wake of the disaster and shared this information with the government and UN agencies to assist their relief efforts. The Data Collaborative between NCEL and Flowminder allowed humanitarian organisations to better target aid to affected communities—saving many lives. While there is great potential and promise for data sharing, Verhulst (2021) highlighted that collaborating with data is one of the main challenges that (big) data initiatives for public good currently face.

As part of the appendix, we highlight some examples of resources and tools about data sharing that could be used by non-profits to find more information and examples, including example data sharing agreements.

Key Takeaways from This Chapter

In this chapter, we aimed to move beyond a rationale for non-profits getting involved in data analytics (Chap. 1) and illustrating how this can be done (Chap. 2). We explored data capability, a collaborative data action methodology, data governance, ethics and consent. The key points to take away from this chapter are presented below.

> **Key Takeaways**
>
> - Data capability for non-profits is a holistic resource that involves interconnected aspects of appropriate staff roles and skills, technologies and data management practices and processes that match needs, mission and strategy. It isn't static because it changes in relation to context, work and goals.
> - Collaborating in data projects (collaborative data action) is a way to build data capability and to learn what is needed to achieve data capability. It is useful because it targets real challenges of participating organisations or departments and brings together varied expertise and different perspectives on challenges.
> - Putting in place a sound data governance system is vital for managing data responsibly, legally and ethically and underpins a shared organisational data culture. More than a set of processes, it involves strategic thinking about relationships between a non-profit and its consumers, clients, customers and communities.
> - Laws governing consent and access to data in jurisdictions are significant to working ethically. Alongside this, formulating consent and data sharing processes ideally involves co-design, including with people represented in the data.

The next and last chapter reflects on overall learnings, gives practical advice about starting or proceeding, and looks to the future and its challenges and possibilities.

References

Alhassan, I., Sammon, D., & Daly, M. (2018). Data governance activities: A comparison between scientific and practice-oriented literature. *Journal of Enterprise Information Management, 31*(2), 300–316. https://doi.org/10.1108/JEIM-01-2017-0007

Arena, O., & Hendey, L. (2019). *A look at the diversity of NNIP*. National Neighborhood Indicators Partnership, Urban Institute. Retrieved April 14, 2022, from https://www.neighborhoodindicators.org/sites/default/files/publications/A%20Look%20at%20the%20Diversity%20of%20NNIP_FINAL.pdf

Benfeldt, O., Persson, J. S., & Madsen, S. (2020). Data governance as a collective action problem. *Information Systems Frontiers, 22*(2), 299–313. https://doi.org/10.1007/s10796-019-09923-z

DAMA International. (2017). *DAMA-DMBOK: Data management body of knowledge*. Technics Publications.

Data Orchard. (2019). *Data maturity framework for the not-for-profit sector* (Version 2). Retrieved April 14, 2022, from https://www.dataorchard.org.uk/resources/data-maturity-framework

European Parliament, & the Council of the European Union. (2016). REGULATION (EU) 2016/679 OF THE EUROPEAN PARLIAMENT AND OF THE COUNCIL of 27 April 2016 on the protection of natural persons with regard to the processing of personal data and on the free movement of such data, and repealing Directive 95/46/EC (General Data Protection Regulation). Official Journal of the European Union, L199/1–L119/88. Retrieved April 14, 2022, from https://eur-lex.europa.eu/eli/reg/2016/679/oj

Franzke, A. S., Muis, I., & Schäfer, M. T. (2021). Data Ethics Decision Aid (DEDA): A dialogical framework for ethical inquiry of AI and data projects in the Netherlands. *Ethics and Information Technology, 23*, 551–567. https://doi.org/10.1007/s10676-020-09577-5

Governance Institute of Australia. (2022). *What is governance?* Retrieved January 19, 2022, from https://www.governanceinstitute.com.au/resources/what-is-governance/

Hardinges, J., & Keller, J. R. (2022). *What are data institutions and why are they important?* The Open Data Institute. Retrieved March 29, 2022, from https://theodi.org/article/what-are-data-institutions-and-why-are-they-important/#:~:text=Data%20institutions%20are%20organisations%20that,into%20our%20theory%20of%20change

Hendey, L., Pettit, K. L. S., Cowan, J., & Gaddy, M. (2020). *Investing in data capacity for community change*. Urban Institute. Retrieved April 14, 2022, from https://www.urban.org/sites/default/files/publication/102347/investing-in-data-capacity-for-community-change_1_1.pdf

Kukutai, T., & Taylor, J. (Eds.). (2016). *Indigenous data sovereignty: Toward an agenda*. ANU Press.

Mittelstadt, B. D., & Floridi, L. (2016). The ethics of big data: Current and foreseeable issues in biomedical contexts. *Science and Engineering Ethics, 22*(2), 303–341. https://doi.org/10.1007/s11948-015-9652-2

Murray, B., Falkenberger, E., & Saxena, P. (2015). *Data walks: An innovative way to share data with communities*. Urban Institute. Retrieved April 14,

2022, from https://www.urban.org/research/publication/data-walks-innovative-way-share-data-communities

National Neighborhood Indicators Partnership. (2018). *NNIP lessons on local data sharing*. Retrieved April 14, 2022, from https://www.neighborhoodindicators.org/library/guides/nnip-lessons-local-data-sharing

NESTA. (2022). *Data analytics*. Retrieved August 5, 2022, from https://www.nesta.org.uk/project/data-analytics/

Open Data Institute. (2019). *Data ethics canvas*. Retrieved January 18, 2022, from https://www.theodi.org/wp-content/uploads/2019/07/ODI-Data-Ethics-Canvas-2019-05.pdf

Otto, B. (2011). Organizing data governance: Findings from the telecommunications industry and consequences for large service providers. *Communications of the Association for Information Systems, 29*, 3. https://doi.org/10.17705/1CAIS.02903

Perkmann, M., & Schildt, H. (2014). Open data partnerships between firms and universities: The role of boundary organizations. *Research Policy, 44*(5), 1133–1143. https://doi.org/10.1016/j.respol.2014.12.006

Redden, J., Brand, J., & Terzieva, V. (2020). *Data Harm Record (Updated)*. Retrieved January 19, 2022, from https://datajusticelab.org/data-harm-record/

Rosenbaum, S. (2010). Data governance and stewardship: Designing data stewardship entities and advancing data access. *Health Services Research, 45*(5p2), 1442–1455. https://doi.org/10.1111/j.1475-6773.2010.01140.x

Sangwan, S. (2021, April 27). How to know you are a 'data intermediary' under the Data Governance Act. *The Privacy Advisor*. https://iapp.org/news/a/how-to-know-you-are-a-data-intermediary-under-the-data-governance-act/

Susha, I., Janssen, M., & Verhulst, S. (2017). Data collaboratives as a new frontier of cross-sector partnerships in the age of open data: Taxonomy development. *Proceedings of the 50th Hawaii International Conference on System Sciences* 2017, Waikoloa Village, Hawaii, United States. https://doi.org/10.24251/HICSS.2017.325

The GovLab. (n.d.). *Phase 1: Demand*. Retrieved April 14, 2022, from https://datacollaboratives.org/canvas.html

Tripp, W., Gage, D., & Williams, H. (2020). Addressing the data analytics gap: A community university partnership to enhance analytics capabilities in the non-profit sector. *Collaborations: A Journal of Community-Based Research and Practice, 3*(1), 11. https://doi.org/10.33596/coll.58

UK Data Service. (2017). *What is the Five Safes frameworks?* Retrieved January 18, 2022, from https://ukdataservice.ac.uk/help/secure-lab/what-is-the-five-safes-framework/

Verhulst, S. G. (2021). Reimagining data responsibility: 10 new approaches toward a culture of trust in re-using data to address critical public needs. *Data & Policy, 3*, e6. https://doi.org/10.1017/dap.2021.4

Verhulst, S. G., & Sangokoya, D. (2015). *Data collaboratives: Exchanging data to improve people's lives*. Retrieved April 14, 2022, from https://sverhulst.medium.com/data-collaboratives-exchanging-data-to-improve-peoples-lives-d0fcfc1bdd9a

Verhulst, S. G., Young, A., Zahuranec, A. J., Aaronson, S. A., Calderon, A., & Gee, M. (2020). The emergence of a third wave of open data. *Open Data Policy Lab*. Retrieved April 14, 2022, from https://apo.org.au/node/311570

Williams, S. (2020). *Data action: Using data for public good*. MIT Press.

Yao, X., McCosker, A., Albury, K., Maddox, A., & Farmer, J. (2021). Building data capacity in the not-for-profit sector: Interim report. *Swinburne University of Technology*. Retrieved April 14, 2022, from https://apo.org.au/node/314477

Open Access This chapter is licensed under the terms of the Creative Commons Attribution 4.0 International License (http://creativecommons.org/licenses/by/4.0/), which permits use, sharing, adaptation, distribution and reproduction in any medium or format, as long as you give appropriate credit to the original author(s) and the source, provide a link to the Creative Commons licence and indicate if changes were made.

The images or other third party material in this chapter are included in the chapter's Creative Commons licence, unless indicated otherwise in a credit line to the material. If material is not included in the chapter's Creative Commons licence and your intended use is not permitted by statutory regulation or exceeds the permitted use, you will need to obtain permission directly from the copyright holder.

4

Activating for a Data-Capable Future

So far in this book, we have argued for non-profits building their capability for working with data. We have presented a range of small, practical data projects with non-profits undertaken through our research in 2017–2022. These supported participating non-profits to build aspects of their data capability by helping leaders and staff to consider the skills, technologies and management practices that would be needed to match their different missions and contexts. We used a *collaborative data action methodology* that draws on diverse skills and experiences within and across organisations, enabling people to learn in practical situations. Projects generated new insights about social challenges, communities and the value of internal organisational data. This made collaborating with data a journey of surprises and creativity as well as a journey of learning.

In this final chapter, we return to our initial idea of giving a rationale for data capability in the non-profit sector, suggesting benefits and stages. In the middle, we give some activities to 'take to your manager' to get started, and thereafter to move beyond an initial data project. We also suggest some strategic actions at organisation, sector and funder levels that would help to make data analytics part of a new 'business as usual'. The latter part looks to the future and considers how emergent data initiatives could address current challenges, drawing on some illustrative

© The Author(s) 2023
J. Farmer et al., *Data for Social Good*, https://doi.org/10.1007/978-981-19-5554-9_4

examples. We conclude by reflecting on our learnings from the research and suggest areas for further studies. The content seeks to stimulate but also to reassure. We think achieving high-quality data analytics work targeted at social good is a viable prospect for non-profits; but more than that, we propose it is an essential underpinning for a bright future.

Sectoral Benefits of Non-profits with Data Capability

Throughout this book, we have made various claims for benefits at the *micro-* (individual organisation) through to the *macro-scale* (community, society and sectoral structures) for non-profits building data capability. In this chapter, though, one of our aims is to provide practical material to 'take to your manager' or board. As a first step, we summarise three reasons why non-profits should invest in building data capability: to up-skill for increased organisational competence; to build a more resilient, interconnected non-profit 'field'; and to enable new forms of social justice activism.

Data Capability and Organisational Competence

Let's first check-in on the contention that data capability is a key building block for non-profit organisational competence and agility in the current global environment. Sian Baker, co-Chief Executive of Data Orchard, a UK-based social business, recently stated that many of her consultancy's clients reported that having internal data capability was an essential enabler of their response during the COVID pandemic (Vaux, 2021). For example, UK-based housing service EMH Group was able to rapidly identify their tenants most in need of welfare checks, thanks to a recently enhanced internal database, and the Herefordshire Food Poverty Alliance (UK) used the findings of a 2019 food security risk audit to rapidly provide support to clients in 2020. More widely, there is increasing recognition that government and non-profits need to be able to effectively manage data in order to respond to ongoing social disruptions and disasters caused by public health challenges, climate change and military conflict in our new age of permanent crisis (Social Ventures Australia and the Centre for Social Impact, 2021; Riboldi et al., 2022). In particular, non-profits need to know what data they have, what data they lack, and how their staff can work ethically and effectively with data.

Data Capability and Field-Building

Acknowledging there are wider gains to be had, Riboldi et al.'s (2022) report, capturing post-pandemic Australian non-profit leaders' views, showed a clear consensus for a move away from charismatic and hierarchical leadership practices, towards community engaged, collaborative decision-making. Leaders reflected on the near impossibility of building new partnerships during the COVID-19 crisis, pointing to the significance of being able to leverage "pre-existing relationships, data and insights" when reaching out to government agencies for funding and support (Riboldi et al., 2022, p. 97). Collective working has long been urged for the non-profit sector (Austin and Seitanidi, 2012; Butcher, 2014). Working with data can be a driver and underpinning structure for non-profit collaborations. In our projects we have shown multiple ways and levels that data projects work to build collaborations (see Chaps. 2 and 3).

Working collaboratively to harness and activate data resources can help to build preparedness and resilience for crises by generating good quality data pools. It can draw stakeholders together to learn how to work with each other and to build social capital. Discussing the idea of *field-building*, McLeod Grant et al. (2020) note that non-profits need to collaborate so that bigger and stronger organisations can support smaller and niche non-profits. This will help to keep the sector diverse and able to meet nuanced needs of different groups and contexts. Resolving social challenges needs a range of organisations to work together as no single organisation can resolve complex social challenges. The field needs to join forces on infrastructure and capabilities so it can afford to do the formidable job it needs to achieve (McLeod Grant et al., 2020). Collaborating with data can be a catalyst and enabler for wider collaboration.

Data Capability and Social Justice Activism

We also want to acknowledge and promote the potential of data analytics for social good as social justice activism. This takes non-profits' data work into a space beyond using it to resolve their own operational challenges. It seeks data work that positively spills over into activating social change in the community (Maddison & Scalmer, 2006). In this sense, non-profits could *apply* their data capability, access to multiple datasets and knowledge generated from analysing datasets. They could direct these resources to advocate for marginalised people within social policy processes and to enable citizens themselves to be active with data, through spreading digital and data skills. Here, we are saying that by engaging citizens to work with data, non-profits can empower them with data skills, and with access to new knowledge assets about their communities. Data for social good as activism aligns with Williams' (2020) depiction of social data projects as *data action*. She explains activism as being about inclusion of diverse participants, including citizens, tackling social challenges using different datasets and about ground-truthing with grassroots perspectives. Wells (2020) also highlights the credentials of data for good as social activism, saying "data for good means data for all, prioritizing equity, supporting local leaders, and questioning power dynamics, with ethics as a top priority" (para. 1).

Involving the wider community is crucial to avoid repeating past mistakes involving abuses of data that have led to risk aversion and fear. Making active steps to engage citizens is significant in shifting power dynamics. Here, we draw on distinctions made by community informatics researcher Michael Gurstein (2011), for example, who argued that making data openly available (as in open data initiatives) has tended to merely hand data assets to those already powerful through controlling and running systems. Gurstein pointed out that active steps to engage beyond managers and leaders are vital for empowering marginalised or disadvantaged groups. Similarly, Kitchin (2013) highlighted that money spent on generating accessible re-used data resources is money not spent directly on supporting marginalised citizens. Consequently, access to data must be democratised and citizens actively empowered to engage with data and inform its application. If not, increased forays into data analytics by non-profits might be seen as representing a diversion of scarce resources to bolster power among those who already enjoy it.

Three Stages of Non-profits' Data Capability

Building data capability, then, is significant to non-profits' business competency, field-building and supporting social change. At its most basic, participating in a data project using collaborative data action can be pitched to leaders as an *efficient learning programme* about working with data. It is significant that non-profits should be skilled and knowledgeable about working with data as the sector comes under increasing pressure from funders seeking accountability and from technology corporates and data social businesses seeking market share. Salesforce, for example, a US software company specialising in customer relationship management software, has a suite of products specially for the non-profit sector (Moltzau, 2019). Googling non-profit data analytics produces multiple pages of blogs and news ephemera generated by businesses aiming to persuade non-profits to engage with *their* data products and services. The non-profit sector needs data capability so it does not end up in thrall to Big Tech. Non-profits need know-how so they can be discerning about what is offered and able to ask questions to probe the 'black box' of commercial data products and systems. On the other hand, non-profits need data capability so they can collaborate as a field with government and philanthropic foundation procurers about sensible data generation and reporting.

Given that it could be difficult to convince non-profit leaders, board members or staff to divert resources to building internal data capability, we do not recommend every organisation to jump straight into complex arrangements, like participating in a data collaborative. Nor do we suggest that every non-profit should seek access to open or commercial datasets or undertake deep dives into sensitive data. Instead, building capability could take an incremental, staged approach:

Stage One: Build Organisational Data Capability The individual non-profit organisation builds off its existing data skills, practices and technologies and uses these resources as a launchpad to develop and improve.

Stage Two: Build Sector Data Capability Extending out from internal capability, the organisation engages in data collaborations with others in the non-profit sector. Leaders and staff seek out like-minded collaborators who are interested in similar topics and questions and who hold useful resources.

Stage Three: Build Community Data Capability Clients, consumers and citizens are engaged to work in equitable partnerships with data. Beyond the non-profit and achieving its operational work in better ways, this stage gives potential to actively extend data capability to the community.

Data Analytics as Business as Usual

In Chaps. 2 and 3, we focused on data projects. However, that doesn't show how data analytics can become embedded as part of a new kind of 'business as usual' for non-profits. It doesn't consider *what happens before* and *leading up to* a data project—or what happens *after*. Here, we cover those phases. Looking first at preparing for a data project and then suggesting activities for proceeding after an initial data project has been undertaken.

Getting Started

In our projects, it has sometimes taken multiple discussions before organisations commit to participating in a data project. Where organisations have been quicker to commit, this tends to be facilitated by interactions with one or more enthusiastic organisational *champions*. These participants also often help by pulling together other interested staff and leaders. Undertaking our data projects has given some pointers about what could help a staff member seeking to take this book to their manager to argue for their organisation 'getting into data analytics', perhaps by engaging in a data project. Below are some of those pointers.

See Data Projects as a Way to Learn About (Your) Data Doing a small data project gives non-profits' staff and leaders the opportunity to experiment with data. It allows for dialogue and collaboration with colleagues within an organisation through a novel opportunity to test the creative potential of their own organisation's datasets.

When undertaking practical data projects with non-profits, we tended to find similar concerns at the start. Many of our participants recognised that their organisations had lots of data and that they should or could be doing something with it. However, participants didn't clearly understand what data they had, what data they lacked—and how they might ask questions and answer them with data. Doing a data project, using a collaborative data action methodology, can address these issues through engaging colleagues collaboratively with their data and their own organisation's challenges.

The key benefits for organisations working on practical data projects (such as those in Chap. 2) were that participants learned new hands-on skills for *working with* specific software programmes, statistical models or modes of data visualisation. Much of that learning was about realising they didn't need to become data scientists. Rather, they learned new languages and practices that enabled them to cooperate across silos and specialisms to understand the value of data in their own organisational contexts. This, in turn, allowed participants to assess what was required in their organisation to realise the kind of data capability they needed to build. By involving a range of staff including managers and frontline workers, there was scope for learning about interactions between data and the roles of different staff members, including understanding the benefits of collecting complete datasets and of being clear around consent to use and re-use data.

Identify Internal Data Champions and Collaborators Leadership is a key aspect of a data project. Those seeking to do a data project should make early moves to identify senior organisation champions who can drive it. These people will be the connectors with internal teams as well as working with any external *data collaborators* (i.e., partners that you may have in other organisations). This champion role involves organising meetings and co-ordinating data protocols or brokering any necessary agreements with external data collaborators (including agreements to identify and share data, as discussed in Chap. 3). The role should not be delegated to junior staff unless they have sufficient authority (and time) to undertake these tasks across the duration of the project. While data champions have a lead role, it is significant to have a range of staff involved in data projects. Frontline workers, in particular, will have knowledge of clients and community needs and the ways in which it is feasible to collect and use data.

Identify External Data Collaborators and Resources These data collaborators may be brought together to form the kind of multi-skilled and multi-resourced data analytics teams described in our projects. In Chap. 3 and the appendix, we outlined various policy institutes, university data labs and other types of institutions with experience in *data for social good* projects, and perhaps with access to technology and skilled staff resources. These might act as skilled data collaborators, but a non-profit can also work with other non-profits or other organisations with aligned mission and access to useful skills, resources and perspectives.

Identify Funding Undertaking a data project takes time, commitment and material resources. Whether a non-profit is keen to build internal data capability or collaborate with data scientists and social scientists as in our projects, sufficient funding is essential to ensure that all parties have the time and resources to do the work. The amount of funding required will vary according to the scale and scope of activities. In the projects outlined in Chap. 2, co-funding was provided by our university, philanthropic organisations, national and state government research funding agencies and our non-profit and other organisation partners. The senior researchers provided their time as an 'in-kind' contribution, but this practice is not always supported by universities. Other ways to access expertise could be through volunteer data scientists, as in DataKind projects (see Appendix). Other resources are also required in data projects including computers and software. While this may seem obvious at first glance, we mention these resources because their costs are not always factored into project grant funding applications.

Be Vigilant About Ethics and Inclusion Advocates and researchers globally have been promoting data for social good for nearly a decade. But the leaders in this field (e.g., Williams, 2020) also caution us about the ethical issues associated with data analytics. In Chaps. 1 and 3, we highlighted the importance of having appropriate consent and clarity around what consent is in place before considering what can be done with data. However, there are other concerns embedded even within datasets that should be borne in mind. Expertise in thinking about hidden ethical issues in data should be built into collaborative teams. As Guyan (2022) observes, even the collection of apparently simple demographic data involves decisions around which kinds of data will be collected—for example, regarding gender, sexuality and trans experience. These choices have significant impacts on who is visible within data and thus how communities, organisations and other phenomena will appear when data is analysed. Decisions based on these data will affect how resources and services are allocated. Similarly, ethical questions should be asked regarding the potential unintended consequences of collecting, collating and communicating with data. As Williams puts it, "data are people" (2020, p. 220). Even well-intentioned data projects can cause harm when they are used to justify surveillance or control of those whose data is analysed within them.

Williams (2020) warns against what she terms 'hubris' in data projects asking: "Why do we often think the data analyst can find the right questions to ask without asking those who have in-depth knowledge of the topics we seek to understand?" (p. xvi). As discussed at other points in this book, the centrality of citizens *in* data does suggest that non-profits need to work to include service users in data projects. While there are useful frameworks and approaches to inform this work, including around Indigenous data sovereignty (Carroll et al., 2020) (discussed in Chap. 1), tested methods and approaches for non-profits engaging their clients and consumers with data are a work-in-progress, we suggest. While waiting for ethics and inclusion practices specifically in relation to this field to mature, we recommend taking the advice of Williams (2020). She suggests using the best ethics practices currently available and 'interprets' Zook et al.'s (2017) *ten simple rules for responsible big data research* to provide a list of ethical principles for data action projects (Williams, 2020, p. 93).

Moving Beyond a Data Project: Next Steps

Once one or more experimental data projects have been completed, enthusiasm fired up and initial data capability is built—then what comes after? How might an organisation work to embed data analytics into business as usual?

Investing for ongoing working with data could involve a non-profit adding new specialist staff and technologies or it could involve collaborating with other non-profits and others to access specialists and technologies. Either way, this suggests different ways of future working need to be considered.

It is increasingly suggested that any organisation, whether building their own team of data specialists or collaborating with others, should designate a *data steward* (Verhulst et al., 2020). Data stewards have a lead role in data governance and hold knowledge about an organisation's datasets, how they were collected and how they can be used. Data stewards can work with other organisations' data stewards if data is to be shared or used in data collaboratives. They are significant to generating "a richer institutional environment around data" (Hardinges & Keller, 2022, para. 23). The Open Data Institute further promotes the idea of *data institutions* (Hardinges & Keller, 2022). These can help to support those organisations that don't or can't afford to invest in dedicated data teams. Data institutions are advocated to help to "steward data on behalf of others" and to support data analytics (Hardinges & Keller, 2022, para. 1). They could take a variety of forms including data collaboratives. Working with a data institution implies the idea of a non-profit contributing to and being part of a type of collective data capability resource.

Our *Data Co-op* platform, which we used to enable the data projects described in Chap. 2, can be understood as a data institution (for other examples, see Appendix). The platform represents an expensive collective resource of data science skills, technologies and data management practices (https://datacoop.com.au/). As such, a non-profit can collaborate with us to use the platform to drive their data projects and their routine data analytics work *and/or* non-profits can work together to share data in collaborative projects (as in Case Study 3). Our *Data Co-op* is a cloud-hosted platform developed by our Social Data Analytics (SoDA) Lab in collaboration with four other Australian Universities and with funding from the Australian Research Council. The platform enables researchers and collaborating partners to use secure virtual environments to access, connect, geospatially map and explore correlations between variables in datasets. These secure data environments provide close integration with Microsoft PowerBI data analytics, enabling advanced visualisation of datasets. Much of the data used in our projects is open public data, such as that of the Australian Bureau of Statistics (ABS), but the platform also has a secure data layer that can hold de-identified and encrypted datasets from collaborating organisations.

While working with a data institution is a way for non-profits to extend their data capability, access to data institutions is not ubiquitous across the world, at present. Generating further access to data-institution-like environments, though, is an area where philanthropy could invest to nurture the data for social good movement (Hendey et al., 2020).

Throughout this book, we have argued that building data capability is important for the future of the non-profit sector and supporting social good. However, non-profits are cash-strapped and there are structural barriers to them pooling resources. In this environment, helping to build sectoral non-profit data capability is a prime space for philanthropic foundations seeking to secure the future of social purpose organisations and to promote social innovation. Philanthropy could support a range of small to larger-scale data initiatives that would be impossible for individual non-profits to pursue alone. There are already some examples of philanthropy supporting non-profits' data capability internationally. As an example, *data.org* is funded by the Rockefeller Foundation and the MasterCard Centre for Inclusive Growth in the US to "democratize and reimagine data science to tackle society's greatest challenges and improve lives across the globe" (The Rockefeller Foundation, 2022). In Australia, where we work, this kind of philanthropic investment to build capability in the non-profit sector has tended to happen in small projects (e.g., see Case Study 2, funded by the Melbourne-based Lord Mayor's Charitable Foundation). Part of the challenge is that foundations traditionally tend to target topics or themes rather than capability-building and infrastructure. However, perhaps the pandemic—by shining a spotlight on the value of online services—might spur more action on infrastructure funding by philanthropy as more reports highlight non-profits' technology-related capability gaps (Riboldi et al., 2022; King et al., 2022). Philanthropy could support place-based initiatives among collaborating non-profits like our City of Greater Bendigo Data Collaborative (Case Study 3), and as in the US National Neighborhood Indicators Partnerships (2022), and theme-based initiatives that support organisations to collaborate to tackle social challenges. Non-profits could be supported to work in data collaborations with each other and/or to work with existing or new data institutions.

Innovations to Solve Data Challenges

The previous chapters have raised technical challenges in progressing data analytics that go beyond simply persuading leaders to get involved. Data sharing, for example, has been raised as perhaps the biggest challenge (Verhulst, 2021). The tendency of small experimental projects in the field is also problematical because it raises questions about the scalability of data analytics within the sector. The good news is that there are rapid changes taking place that are relevant to data for social good. At the same time as generating excitement, the sheer amount of potentially relevant innovation means it is hard to keep up with change. It's also hard to judge what might 'stick'. Here, we share a few examples of emerging innovations to highlight the field's dynamism and to highlight the need for critical thinking about the many opportunities. It's hard to tell how quickly, if at all, some innovations could affect non-profits' work with data and in some cases, whether the innovations actually are 'for good'.

Addressing the problem of many small projects, DataKind (an international data science volunteering organisation) has recently established a *Centre of Excellence* to build non-profits' data capability. A key pillar of work is termed *Impact Practices* (Porway, 2019). The idea built from staff of DataKind identifying that many projects they undertake with social services and non-profits are grouped around similar topics or harness similar techniques. With Impact Practices, DataKind aims to compile, make available and form collaborations around data analytics solutions addressing like topics. In this way, rather than each project starting from scratch and working with DataKind to build something new, work in topics can be translated across non-profits targeting the same social challenge. Porway (2019) writes that work is moving from a *project-based model* to a *practice-based model*—featuring portfolios of data science projects by theme. In a blog announcing the new initiative, an example is given of many projects targeting early detection of disease outbreaks. Rather than building multiple small projects, Impact Practices will unite participants to "understand what data is available, and test real prototypes in the field to understand what's really possible" (Porway, 2019, p. 3).

DataKind's work is dedicated to solving problems of the non-profit sector, and it works internationally, suggesting strong potential for Impact Practices to translate to different contexts and sizes of non-profits, potentially widely influencing non-profit data analytics into the near future.

This transferability may be less likely for our next example of innovation, which is targeted at enabling data sharing. As highlighted in Chap. 3, data sharing between organisations is a significant challenge due to each having different arrangements for consent and privacy. Internationally, there are different privacy regulations around secondary use of data varying by country jurisdictions, for example, the EU General Data Protection Regulation (European Parliament and the Council of the European Union, 2016). To address problems of data sharing across government institutions and borders, the UN Committee of Experts on Big Data and Data Science for Official Statistics is running a pilot programme using Privacy Enhancing Technologies (PETs) (The Economist Science & Technology, 2022). Current work is targeting international trade data sharing between five countries' national data agencies. PETs help data providers and data users to safely share information by using encryption and privacy protocols that allow someone to produce useful output data without 'seeing' the input data. They also ensure that anonymity of data will be protected throughout its lifecycle and that outputs cannot be used to 'reverse engineer' the original data (UN PET Lab, 2022).

This technology is exciting, but only recently initiated and occurring between national statistical offices so innovations developed could take a long time to filter down to become a technology that is routinely accessible to non-profits.

Finally, a concern we raise in various places is citizen involvement. We have noted an imperative to have citizens engaged in data governance and data use, but their inclusion can be hindered by fear of discussing data use and lack of easily useable engagement methods. Elsewhere, we've mentioned citizen data sovereignty initiatives—for example, EU-funded project DECODE (https://decodeproject.eu/what-decode.html) that is experimenting with ways citizens can decide what happens with their data (Monge et al., 2022). And we've also mentioned good practice in Indigenous data sovereignty that can guide work with citizens (Carroll et al., 2020). In some countries internationally—in this case, in Australia, where we work—*consumer data rights* laws have been established, ostensibly to enable citizens to understand their data and to use it for their empowerment. The Australian Consumer Data Right (CDR) is suggested to give citizens choice and control over the data that businesses hold about them (Australian Government, 2020). It enables people to transfer their data to another business to find products and services better tailored to their needs (Australian Government, 2022). Unfortunately, though, as highlighted by Goggin et al. (2019), the driver for this Act is actually to generate new data businesses and the way the Act is explained and promoted is directed at business, with little attention to educating and activating consumers in data literacy. As Goggin et al. (2019) conclude: "In Australia, it is notable that efforts to respond to concern [about consumer data rights] have come, not in the context of an overhaul of privacy laws or digital rights generally, but via efforts, by market-oriented policy bodies …" (p. 12).

This is an example of government enthusiasm for data initiatives resulting in the advancement of for-profit data markets in which public data becomes a product that is commercialised by private developers (Bates, 2012). However, it also potentially serves to highlight an opportunity of where non-profits could harness emergent legislation to empower and advocate for consumers. Non-profits need data capability so they can recognise and harness emergent initiatives like consumer data rights legislation and turn them into opportunities to help build citizen data and digital literacy.

The examples of innovations in this section are used to illustrate the ongoing emerging initiatives that are relevant to non-profits' data analytics. They show that current data analytics challenges are likely to be resolved, but it will take time. They also raise the issue of how to keep up with the pace of change and the many disciplines and perspectives that influence it. This further supports the value of collaborating with others, if only simply to have a chance to keep up-to-date with a fast-changing field.

Research Reflections and Next Steps

Our Research Reflections

Taking a step back to reflect on the research you've done in a field over several projects and years is an indulgence in a pressurised funding environment. However, it is important to do as it reveals patterns and sometimes surprises. In this case, having promoted the benefits of cross-disciplinary and multi-perspective working throughout this book, the realisation dawned that this also makes the work quite challenging. One thing that has come to the fore in writing this book is the complexity that arises from trying to meld the positionality of diverse participants and researchers. Positionality considers how your identity influences, and potentially biases, your understanding of and outlook on the context and phenomena you are working with (Bourke, 2014). Having different perspectives in a data project often means that participants have varying expectations and over-layer their learning on pre-existing frameworks and knowledge bases. To illustrate how this works even within our writing team, one of us sees non-profits using data analytics as being a contemporary manifestation of community development. Others in our team are working closely with non-profits and supporting them to organise better for using data, giving a perspective very grounded in operational issues; while our data scientist views the non-profit field as one of intriguing new datasets to which a range of old and emergent analytical techniques can be applied. Acknowledging the positionality challenges even among our writing team has made us realise how difficult it must be to navigate data projects for our multi-disciplinary, multi-department and multi-organisation practice partners. It makes us think that those that enjoy and thrive in these data projects are likely those who can deal with uncertainty, tolerate or be curious about different perspectives and who are prepared to be flexible with their expectations.

A further issue is inherent in this work *as research*. It is *very* practical, and it is highly participative. We have noted in places that it's more like a learning process than research. In terms of defining it as a research approach, it is perhaps most akin to participatory action research (McIntyre, 2007). The processes are fluid and while punctuated by consistent types of steps and activities, as highlighted in Chap. 3, this can make this work hard to write up as research. And these same issues of not being able to pin down the process nor constrain the timeline precisely can be off-putting for non-profits considering working on data projects. They tend to want a defined process, with stipulated timelines and agreed (beforehand) outputs and outcomes. All quite challenging to delineate at the start of the kinds of data projects we outlined in Chap. 2, when you don't know what datasets a non-profit holds or what the consents governing re-use of data might exist.

While these issues about the data projects can make them frustrating and can deter some non-profits from participating, at the same time the challenges are what make the research interesting and exciting. And the need to tolerate fluidity means our partner organisations tend to be a self-selecting group of innovative early adopters, which makes them fun to work with. This is a space of social innovation, after all.

Aligned with the idea of our partner non-profits as enthusiastic innovators, we have experienced a remarkable degree of buy-in to projects once organisations commit to starting. An example of this is participants regularly turning up to data workshops over project timescales lasting 6–18 months. The City of Greater Bendigo data collaborative, for example, continues to meet and discuss data two years after we started. In that project, there is remarkable buy-in—perhaps because the geospatial data visualisations help service providers and businesses to think about the places where they live and work. Participants are able, repeatedly, to bring suggestions as to why phenomena may be 'seen' in the data analyses, help to ground-truth analyses and give suggestions about datasets and topics that could be explored next. Perhaps there is some sense of wonder at the possibility of generating sleek new data products (in their case, a community resilience data dashboard, see https://datacoop.com.au/bendigo/) from previously routine data produced as cross-sectional reports. There is some sense of excitement at unleashing a valuable resource from a previously apparently passive and dull set of spreadsheets.

What Next in Research?

Turning to what next, some topics emerge as obvious targets for research. Bearing in mind this field is about the nexus between non-profits, their work and mission, and data analytics, and not about other data-related fields like computational techniques or data law. Those areas, no doubt, have many research opportunities of their own, but we won't talk about those here.

We think the most significant issue is around working with citizens, consumers, clients and the community. Feasible, easily applied methods for doing this—with and for non-profits—need to be developed and tested and to become industry standards. Non-profits need to build their data capability, so they are confident and skilled in data to engage with consumers and clients in conversations about data *without fear*. In Chap. 1, we talked about how initiatives like the National Neighborhood Indicators Partnership engage people with (largely) open data and how this is a way to build citizen data literacy and community capability (Murray et al., 2015). This suggests that learning and engagement are best done through topic-focused engagement, rather than teaching focused on data literacy skills. Another approach is to work with consumer representative groups that many non-profits already have and start to engage people in conversations about the data they are in, data governance and re-use of data in analyses.

A second area for exploration is the set of issues around the experience of working in non-profits that have data capability; for example, what difference to organisational functioning, client outcomes and staff motivation does having a positive data culture make? As we propose that working collaboratively with data can help to integrate the work of staff and organisations, can this be evidenced robustly, and what are the impacts of better integrated organisations? Ultimately, what we are saying here is that we do not know the impacts on organisational mission and outcomes of having data capability, though we surmise there are benefits. To date, our research has focused on processes of building data capability, but what does that enable? Crudely, what is the difference between a non-profit that has data capability and one that does not? To date, there are data maturity frameworks, but how do differences in data maturity manifest as lived experiences for organisations, staff, clients and consumers? As more non-profits build their data capability, it will be exciting to see how this changes organisational structures and whether it brings together, and helps to build the strength of non-profits as a field—as we propose and hope for.

A final set of research questions sits around the potential for non-profits' using artificial intelligence (AI) and automated decision-making systems as these techniques become more accessible and more used. A recent blog post from Data Orchard, a UK-based data for social good consultancy, suggested that 15% of charities are now using AI (Vaux, 2021). AI demands large datasets, and so it has been suggested that, despite hype around the efficiencies it can enable, only large non-profits are likely to benefit (Bernholz, 2019; Moltzau, 2019). Cases can be found illustrating use of AI for large datasets, including by Greenpeace for donor segmentation, rainforest protection by analysing mobile phone data and case law analysis by human rights lawyers (Moltzau, 2019; Paver, 2021). Alongside this, there is interest in the potential of AI in place-based initiatives. The GovLab's *AI Localism* (https://ailocalism.org/) is a repository of AI case studies generated by cities, regions and global initiatives (Verhulst et al., 2021). Links between growing data capability of non-profits and entry to using AI is an important area to understand as it unfolds. Of interest is what AI might affect, in terms of the structure and nature of the future non-profit sector. Perhaps the efficiencies it enables for large non-profits will serve to drive further corporatisation and 'survival of the biggest'. But perhaps there will be imaginative place or theme-related AI initiatives based on data collaboratives or collective practices, serving to unite and enable AI and advanced data analytics as non-profit field-building. Participatory AI or how to include stakeholders and citizens in designing ethical AI is another area to watch for non-profits (Bondi et al., 2021).

Key Takeaways from This Chapter and Conclusions

In this chapter we explored how non-profits having data capability could impact on the whole sector and society as well as giving some practical steps about what to do next within organisations. We looked at some future directions for data analytics and highlighted areas for future research. Key takeaways from this chapter are presented below.

> **Key Takeaways**
>
> - Building data capability can benefit non-profits by helping to: (1) manage most effectively and show impact; (2) build a 'field' that collaborates with data to tackle social challenges; (3) generate new ways to address social inequity through community data capability and digital inclusion.
> - To influence the manager of a non-profit to engage with data analytics: suggest involvement in a data project as efficient 'learning by doing'; get internal champions and collaborators on board; explore external expert help and resources; identify funding; and include ethics from the start.
> - To extend beyond a data project: identify an organisational *data steward* to oversee internal data resources; and identify *data institutions* that could help to access external support for advanced projects.
> - While there are current technical and legal challenges, innovation is ongoing that may enable scaling-up from experimental to large-scale practices. Allying with a data institution could help to keep up with change.
> - Key areas for future research are engaging clients and citizens in non-profits' data work; examining impacts of data capability on organisational performance and impact; and use of AI by non-profits.

This chapter concludes this book in which we set out to propose that any non-profit can engage with data for social good and build their data capability. While there are many challenges in this space, we hope this book makes it seem entirely doable. We also hope that while this new capability will help with non-profits' business competitiveness, it can also be experienced as a space where people work together to find creativity and enlightenment.

With its many initiatives, active and high-profile advocates (e.g., Sir Tim Berners-Lee as co-director of the Open Data Institute), data for social good could be described as almost an industry in itself now. Through collaboration and experimenting with data, we suggest that all non-profits should get inside this big tent. We end with a plea—we ask non-profits to beware getting picked off as individual organisations by commercial businesses selling their proprietary data systems. We urge staff and managers instead to get knowledgeable, get skilled, make collaborating 'data friends' of other non-profits and their staff, and to develop their organisation's data capability. This will drive the non-profit sector's data capability for good into the future. Most of all, we suggest people should just get started with working with data and experimental data projects. We urge non-profits to have fun with data in ways that simultaneously help to do (more) good with data.

References

Austin, J. E., & Seitanidi, M. M. (2012). Collaborative value creation: A review of partnering between nonprofits and businesses: Part I. Value creation spectrum and collaboration stages. *Nonprofit and Voluntary Sector Quarterly, 41*(5), 726–758. https://doi.org/10.1177/0899764012450777

Australian Government. (2020). Competition and consumer (consumer data right) rules 2020. *Federal Register of Legislation*. Retrieved April 15, 2022, from https://www.legislation.gov.au/Details/F2021C00076

Australian Government. (2022). What is the consumer data right? *Office of the Australian Information Commissioner*. Retrieved April 15, 2022, from https://www.oaic.gov.au/consumer-data-right/what-is-the-consumer-data-right?msclkid=6e0c2c04af0311ecaaef2291d1e29ba1

Bates, J. (2012). "This is what modern deregulation looks like": Co-optation and contestation in the shaping of the UK's Open Government Data Initiative. *The Journal of Community Informatics, 8*(2), 1–20. https://doi.org/10.15353/joci.v8i2.3038

Bernholz, L. (2019). Nonprofits and AI. *LinkedIn*. Retrieved April 19, 2022, from https://www.linkedin.com/pulse/nonprofits-ai-lucy-bernholz/

Bondi, E., Xu, L., Acosta-Navas, D., & Killian, J. A. (2021). Envisioning communities: A participatory approach towards AI for social good. *Proceedings of the 2021 AAAI/ACM Conference on AI, Ethics, and Society*, pp. 425–436. https://doi.org/10.1145/3461702.3462612

Bourke, B. (2014). Positionality: Reflecting on the research process. *The Qualitative Report, 19*(33), 1–9. https://doi.org/10.46743/2160-3715/2014.1026

Butcher, J. (2014). Does size really matter? Big charity and civil society at a Crossroads. *ResearchGate*. Retrieved April 15, 2022, from https://www.researchgate.net/publication/297543180_Does_size_really_matter_Big_charity_and_civil_society_at_a_Crossroads

Carroll, S. R., Garba, I., Figueroa-Rodríguez, O. L., Holbrook, J., Lovett, R., Materechera, S., Parsons, M., Raseroka, K., Rodriguez-Lonebear, D., Rowe, R., Sara, R., Walker, J. D., Anderson, J., & Hudson, M. (2020). The CARE principles for indigenous data governance. *Data Science Journal, 19*(1), 43. https://doi.org/10.5334/dsj-2020-043

European Parliament and the Council of the European Union. (2016). REGULATION (EU) 2016/679 OF THE EUROPEAN PARLIAMENT AND OF THE COUNCIL of 27 April 2016 on the protection of natural persons with regard to the processing of personal data and on the free movement of such data, and repealing Directive 95/46/EC (General Data Protection Regulation). Official Journal of the European Union, L199/1-L119/88. Retrieved April 7, 2022, from http://eurlex.europa.eu/eli/reg/2016/679/oj

Goggin, G., Vromen, A., Weatherall, K., Martin, F., & Sunman, L. (2019). Data and digital rights: Recent Australian developments. *Internet Policy Review, 8*(1). https://doi.org/10.14763/2019.1.1390

Gurstein, M. B. (2011). Open data: Empowering the empowered or effective data use for everyone? *First Monday*. Retrieved April 15, 2022, https://firstmonday.org/article/view/3316/2764

Guyan, K. (2022). *Queer data: Using gender, sex and sexuality data for action.* Bloomsbury Publishing.

Hardinges, J., & Keller J. R. (2022). What are data institutions and why are they important? *The Open Data Institute*. Retrieved March 29, 2022, from https://theodi.org/article/what-are-data-institutions-and-why-are-they-important/#:~:text=Data%20institutions%20are%20organisations%20that,into%20our%20theory%20of%20change

Hendey, L., Pettit, K. L. S., Cowan, J., & Gaddy, M. (2020). *Investing in data capacity for community change*. Urban Institute. Retrieved April 15, 2022, from https://www.urban.org/sites/default/files/publication/102347/investing-in-data-capacity-for-community-change_1_1.pdf

King, D., Chan, O., Coule, T., Dahill, D., Mainard-Sardon, J., Martin, A., Rossiter, W., Smith, S., Stuart, J., Vahidi, G., & Ibokessien, N. (2022). Respond, recover, reset: Two years on. *Nottingham Trent University, Centre for People, Work and Organisational Practice*. Retrieved April 15, 2022, from https://www.ntu.ac.uk/__data/assets/pdf_file/0029/1673741/Respond-Recover-Reset-Two-Years-On-2022.pdf

Kitchin, R. (2013). Four critiques of open data initiatives. *LSE Impact Blog*. Retrieved April 15, 2020, from https://blogs.lse.ac.uk/impactofsocialsciences/2013/11/27/four-critiques-of-open-data-initiatives/#:~:text=Consequently%2C%20as%20a%20provocation%20for,the%20benign%20and%20empowers%20the

Maddison, S., & Scalmer, S. (2006). *Activist wisdom: Practical knowledge and creative tension in social movements*. UNSW Press.

McIntyre, A. (2007). *Participatory action research*. Sage Publications.

McLeod Grant, H., Wilkinson, K., & Butts, M. (2020). Building capacity for sustained collaboration. *Stanford Social Innovation Review*. https://doi.org/10.48558/V5BG-2308

Moltzau, A. (2019). Artificial intelligence and non-profits: How can non-profits use AI for good? *Towards Data Science*. Retrieved April 19, 2022, from https://towardsdatascience.com/artificial-intelligence-and-nonprofit-e6cdaaae166f

Monge, F., Barns, S., Kattel, R., & Bria, F. (2022). *A new data deal: The case of Barcelona (Working Paper Series No. WP 2022/02)*. UCL Institute for Innovation and Public Purpose. Retrieved March 21, 2022, from https://www.ucl.ac.uk/bartlett/public-purpose/wp2022-02

Murray, B., Falkenberger, E., & Saxena, P. (2015). *Data walks: An innovative way to share data with communities*. Urban Institute. Retrieved April 4, 2022, from https://www.urban.org/research/publication/data-walks-innovative-way-share-data-communities

National Neighborhood Indicators Partnership. (2022). *About NNIP*. Retrieved October 13, 2022, from https://www.neighborhoodindicators.org/about-nnip

Paver, C. (2021). Artificial intelligence for non-profits. *Dataro*. Retrieved April 19, 2022, from https://dataro.io/2021/03/09/artificial-intelligence-for-nonprofits/#:~:text=How%20do%20nonprofits%20use%20AI,the%20 guesswork%20out%20of%20segmentation

Porway, J. (2019). Creating a systems change approach for data science and AI solutions. *DataKind*. Retrieved April 15, 2022, from https://www.datakind.org/blog/creating-a-systems-change-approach-for-data-science-ai-solutions

Riboldi, M., Fennis, L., & Stears, M. (2022). *Nurturing links across civil society: Lessons from Australia's for-purpose sector's response to COVID-19*. Sydney Policy Lab, University of Sydney. Retrieved April 15, 2022, from https://apo.org.au/node/316831

Social Ventures Australia and the Centre for Social Impact. (2021). *Vital support: Building resilient charities to support Australia's wellbeing*. Retrieved April 7, 2022, from https://www.socialventures.com.au/work/vital-support-building-resilient-charities-to-support-australias-wellbeing/

The Economist Science & Technology. (2022, January 29). The UN is testing technology that processes data confidentially. *The Economist*. Retrieved March 29, 2022, from https://www.economist.com/science-and-technology/the-un-is-testing-technology-that-processes-data-confidentially/21807385?msclkid=8214e306aef811ec8453ee433632f753

The Rockefeller Foundation. (2022). Data.org. Retrieved April 15, 2022, from https://www.rockefellerfoundation.org/initiative/data-org/

UN PET Lab. (2022). *UN launches first of its kind 'privacy lab' to unlock benefits of international data sharing*. Retrieved March 29, 2022, from https://unstats.un.org/bigdata/events/2022/unsc-un-pet-lab/UN%20PET%20Lab%20-%20Press%20Release%20-%2025%20Jan%202022.pdf

Vaux, H. (2021). Data maturity and how it helps charities achieve their broader objectives. *Zoe Amar Digital*. Retrieved August 4, 2022, from https://zoeamar.com/2021/12/09/data-maturity/?utm_source=Mailing+list+-+Data4Good&utm_campaign=11ccbe47a4-Newsletter-Dec2021&utm_medium=email&utm_term=0_c5dbb57baa-11ccbe47a4-375145142&mc_cid=11ccbe47a4&mc_eid=9cb417af82

Verhulst, S., Young, A., & Sloane, M. (2021). The AI localism canvas: A framework to assess the emergence of governance of AI within cities. Informationen zur Raumentwicklung, 48(3), 86–88. Retrieved April 20, 2022, from https://elibrary.steiner-verlag.de/article/99.105010/izr202103008601

Verhulst, S. G. (2021). Reimagining data responsibility: 10 new approaches toward a culture of trust in re-using data to address critical public needs. *Data & Policy*, *3*, e6. https://doi.org/10.1017/dap.2021.4

Verhulst, S. G., Zahuranec, A. J., Young, A., & Winowatan, M. (2020). Wanted: Data stewards: (Re-)defining the roles and responsibilities of data stewards for an age of data collaboration. *The GovLab*. Retrieved April 15, 2022, from https://thegovlab.org/static/files/publications/wanted-data-stewards.pdf

Wells, R. (2020). Introducing DataKind's Center of Excellence. *DataKind*. Retrieved April 15, 2022, from https://www.datakind.org/blog/introducing-datakinds-center-of-excellence

Williams, S. (2020). *Data action: Using data for public good*. MIT Press.

Zook, M., Barocas, S., Boyd, D., Crawford, K., Keller, E., Gangadharan, S. P., Goodman, A., Hollander, R., Koenig, B. A., Metcalf, J., & Narayanan, A. (2017). Ten simple rules for responsible big data research. *PLoS Computational Biology, 13*(3), e1005399. https://doi.org/10.1371/journal.pcbi.1005399

Open Access This chapter is licensed under the terms of the Creative Commons Attribution 4.0 International License (http://creativecommons.org/licenses/by/4.0/), which permits use, sharing, adaptation, distribution and reproduction in any medium or format, as long as you give appropriate credit to the original author(s) and the source, provide a link to the Creative Commons licence and indicate if changes were made.

The images or other third party material in this chapter are included in the chapter's Creative Commons licence, unless indicated otherwise in a credit line to the material. If material is not included in the chapter's Creative Commons licence and your intended use is not permitted by statutory regulation or exceeds the permitted use, you will need to obtain permission directly from the copyright holder.

Appendix: The Data Innovation Ecosystem and Its Resources

Initiatives

Initiatives in different countries are progressing innovations relevant to data analytics for non-profits. Figure A.1 shows some types of initiatives in the ecosystem and the range of goals they are aiming to achieve. A recent taxonomy of AI and data for social good from *data.org* provides an extended map of initiatives in the landscape.[1]

Below, we list some examples of the key types of initiatives. Later in this section, we also outline some of the kinds of resources and support available from these. There are many examples of initiatives, they exist around the world and new initiatives keep emerging, so this list is by no means comprehensive. We focused on initiatives and resources *that we have used* and that influenced our work to date.

---

[1] Porway, J. (2022). A taxonomy for AI/data for good. *Data.org*. Retrieved March 21, 2022, from https://data.org/news/a-taxonomy-for-ai-data-for-good/.

114   Appendix: The Data Innovation Ecosystem and Its Resources

Fig. A.1   Initiatives and goals of the non-profits' data innovation ecosystem

Think Tanks and Policy Institutes

The GovLab (https://thegovlab.org/) is a policy institute based at New York University that targets capability-building for public sector governance and has developed pioneering models and tools around data governance and re-use; for example, *datacollaboratives.org* has a methodology and a portal to host international data collaboratives (https://datacollaboratives.org/).

Both *The GovLab* (US) and *NESTA* (UK) (https://nesta.org.uk/project/data-analytics/) undertake demonstrator and experimental projects to push the boundaries of social data analytics practice and establish standards. Advocating for use of data for social good, they sometimes work with partner organisations including non-profits and have wider goals as 'data institutions'[2] to leave a practical legacy including

---

[2] Hardinges, J., & Keller, J. R. (2022). *What are data institutions and why are they important?* The Open Data Institute. Retrieved March 29, 2022, from https://theodi.org/article/what-are-data-institutions-and-why-are-they-important/#:~:text=Data%20institutions%20are%20organisations%20that,into%20our%20theory%20of%20change.

tools and data capability. Much of the work of these organisations is funded via philanthropic foundations, governments or corporates.

Specifically targeting non-profits, the *Stanford University Digital Civil Society Lab* (https://pacscenter.stanford.edu/research/digital-civil-society-lab/) has a repository of useful tools to increase data analytics capability, generated from high-quality projects.

Some initiatives are focused on building capability of citizens and communities—for example, the Washington DC-based Urban Institute's *National Neighborhood Indicators Partnership* (NNIP) (https://www.neighborhoodindicators.org/) has a mission "to ensure all communities have access to data and the skills to use information to advance equity and well-being across neighborhoods".[3] The focus is on using suburb or community-level data and engaging local citizens, services and non-profits together to inform local decision-making and empower through democratizing information.

The NNIP supports organisations at city and region level to codesign community indicators with citizens and to train local people as citizen scientists to gather neighbourhood data to ground truth analyses based on open public data.[4] One example, drawn from the NNIP online case studies library, illustrates how community-based data projects work. The City of Oakland, US, developed a new strategy for addressing violence in the community. Existing city administrative data about reported crime, gang activity and domestic violence was analysed. Simultaneously, 16 community residents were trained to collect data about local lived experiences. Based on analyses of quantitative city data and qualitative evidence about experiences, citizens and city staff generated data-driven ideas for the new strategy, including re-evaluating gun violence prevention programmes and using trauma-informed principles.

Neighborhood Partnerships and their projects are typically funded by multiple participating organisations and philanthropy.

Other significant policy institutes and think tanks include the Open Data Institute (https://theodi.org/), the Ada Lovelace Institute—funded

---

[3] National Neighborhood Indicators Partnership. (2022). *NNIP Mission*. Retrieved March 21, 2022, from https://www.neighborhoodindicators.org/about-nnip/nnip-mission.

[4] National Neighborhood Indicators Partnership. (2022). *NNIP Mission*. Retrieved March 21, 2022, from https://www.neighborhoodindicators.org/about-nnip/nnip-mission.

by the Nuffield Foundation in the UK (https://www.adalovelaceinstitute.org/) and the Data Justice Lab at Cardiff University, Wales (https://datajusticelab.org/).

Data Science Volunteering

This kind of initiative harnesses the power of data scientists who volunteer their skills to work with socially oriented organisations to explore the potential of using data—often via hackathons and projects. *DataKind* (https://www.datakind.org/) is one such organisation, operating through franchised 'chapters' in the UK, the US, India and Singapore. DataKind has established criteria that prospective data projects must meet in order to access volunteer help and access to the DataKind methodology. Once a data project is accepted, DataKind works through a set of steps with organisations to identify datasets, imagine useful data solutions and then to work through processes to prototype suitable solutions. One criterion for participation in DataKind projects is that the organisation will be able to maintain the data solution beyond the initial project. This suggests some pre-existing data capability is needed—although discussions on the DataKind website, giving feedback from different projects, suggest DataKind projects are good opportunities for non-profits to learn and extend knowledge.

As an example, DataKind volunteers worked with a UK food bank to develop a machine-learning model that predicts which clients will be highest users, allowing the food bank to prioritise these citizens for additional support.

University Social Data Analytics Labs

Universities around the world may be particularly well-placed to work with non-profits on practical collaborative projects that foster experimentation and growth of data capability. This is partly because universities are experienced in bringing together expertise from across disciplines and in facilitating partnerships across research and practice boundaries.⁵ Some have social data analytics labs for research and development and to give data science students experience of working with non-profits. Examples include Auckland University Centre for Social Data Analytics, New Zealand; University of West Georgia Data Analysis and Visualization Lab, US; and our Social Data Analytics Lab at Swinburne University of Technology, Melbourne Australia (https://www.swinburne.edu.au/research/institutes/social-innovation/social-data-analytics-lab/).

Demonstrator Projects

Large funding bodies can generate demonstrator projects to trial new ideas and solutions. One such large project is the European Union-funded Project DECODE (DEcentralised Citizen-owned Data Ecosystems; see https://decodeproject.eu/). It focuses on exploring citizen data sovereignty practices, with demonstrator sites in cities including Barcelona and Amsterdam.⁶

Socially Oriented Data Consultancies and Businesses

For-profit and social businesses have emerged that work with non-profits and other organisations to generate tools and re-used data resources. Examples of businesses include Data Orchard (UK), a non-profit consultancy that developed a Data Maturity Framework for non-profits to assess organisational progress in data capability (see https://www.dataorchard.org.uk/); Seer Data and Analytics (Australia) that works with non-profits and communities to design data dashboards for community development (see https://seerdata.ai/); and Neighbourlytics (Australia) that re-uses data generated by social media and sharing platforms to

---

⁵ Tripp, W., Gage, D., & Williams, H. (2020). Addressing the data analytics gap: A community university partnership to enhance analytics capabilities in the non-profit sector. *Collaborations: A Journal of Community-Based Research and Practice*, 3(1), 1–10. https://doi.org/10.33596/coll.58.

⁶ Monge, F., Barns, S., Kattel, R., & Bria, F. (2022). *A new data deal: The case of Barcelona* (Working Paper Series No. WP 2022/02). UCL Institute for Innovation and Public Purpose. Retrieved March 21, 2022, from https://www.ucl.ac.uk/bartlett/public-purpose/wp2022-02.

provide analyses about social characteristics of places (see https://neighbourlytics.com/).

Initiatives with Government Funding

There are some government initiatives that can be accessed for ideas and potentially partnerships and grant funding, for example, The Data Lab (https://thedatalab.com/) has a mission to "help Scotland maximise value from data and lead the world to a data powered future".[7] It supports businesses of all kinds to use data, helps to run courses, and supports studentships and student placements. It is funded by the Scottish Funding Council as part of its Innovation Centres programme.

Useful Resources for Non-Profits Developing Data Projects

There are many existing resources and tools that can be drawn on for examples and guidance when considering specific aspects of data projects and building capability. Table A.1 highlights some examples we have drawn on in our work. New resources and tools are frequently being developed.

---

[7] The Data Lab. (2022). *The Data Lab is Scotland's Innovation Centre for data and AI*. Retrieved April 14, 2022, from https://thedatalab.com.

Table A.1 Tools and guides from existing initiatives

Initiative and its focus	Tools and guides about these topics						
	Contracts	Data governance and management	Skills	Ethics and consent	Data sharing	Working with citizens	Curated collections
Digital Civil Society Lab, Stanford University, US Digital civil society and philanthropy	• Templates for data contracts	• Digital impact toolkit • Data inventory • Organisational policy inventory • Data governance workbook	• Digital organisational chart • How to hire a data expert guide	• Templates for consent			• Tools and templates specifically for non-profits and data
National Neighborhood Indicators Partnership, Urban Institute, US Building community data capacity		• Data management practices • Data governance tools and guides • Data usability guide			• Data sharing, storage and consent guide	• Reports on: Data walks; Engaging communities, etc.	
DataKind, US, UK, Singapore, India Data philanthropy and volunteering		• Center of excellence • DataKind playbook		• Practitioners guide to data ethics			
Open Data Institute, UK Equitable access to data innovation		• Data toolkit for business	• Explainers and guides on skills	• Ethics canvas	• Explainers and guides on data sharing • Open standards for health data sharing		

(*continued*)

Table A.1 (continued)

Initiative and its focus	Tools and guides about these topics						
	Contracts	Data governance and management	Skills	Ethics and consent	Data sharing	Working with citizens	Curated collections
Data Justice Lab, Wales. Data and social justice, digital citizenship						• Guidebook with examples of methods	
Ada Lovelace Institute, UK. Ethical and societal impacts of data and AI						• Guide to citizen participation in data use	
NESTA, UK. Data analytics in health, labour markets and creative arts		• Map the Gap tool to map data challenges			• Data sharing toolkit		
Governance Lab at New York University				• Data responsibility framework	• Data sharing tools and methodologies		
Datacollaboratives.org, US	• Example contracts for data collaboration						• Tools for data re-use
Strengthening institutions through better use of data							

Glossary[1]

AI (artificial intelligence) Use of computer-controlled techniques to analyse large datasets to discover new insights, patterns and relationships in data.

Collaborative data action The practice of experimenting and discovering with data, involving data collaborators, perhaps from different departments of an organisation or from different organisations. Collaborative data action involves bringing different skills and backgrounds together to apply data analytics for new insights and learning.

Data analytics The process of generating data and examining it to find patterns and insights that can aid decision-making and offer courses of action.

Data capability A holistic concept involving having the right skills, technologies and data management practices for your non-profit organisation's size, mission and context. Data capability of non-profits will change over time as they get more experienced and want to do more with data—that is, data capability is situated and should meld and flex in relation to context. The term 'data capacity' is sometimes used interchangeably with data capability.

Data capacity See data capability above.

---

[1] This glossary gives our understanding of terms as we use them in this book.

Glossary

Data collaboration Where different participants work together with data, perhaps across an organisation's departments or across a range of organisations. This type of collaboration could be formalised in a data collaborative.

Data collaborative A formal arrangement or type of project where organisations or entities agree to work together for data sharing.

Data collaborators People or entities that work with you in your data project or collaboration. Typically, different data collaborators may bring different resources to a project, such as data science skills or non-profit practice experience. Data collaborators may be from different organisations or departments working together in a data collaboration.

Data co-op We use this term to include situations where organisations co-operate together, with their data, to address a social mission. The term is also applied to situations where citizens co-operate to apply their own data for causes they select.

Data dashboard An interactive data visualisation tool that provides ability to filter, search and explore different aspects of a dataset.

Data for social good Application of contemporary data science techniques to datasets to address a social mission or question.

Data governance The systems and processes so that an organisation can ensure data is managed and analysed responsibly, legally and ethically.

Data institution Organisations that work to support non-profits, communities and others to work more actively with data, often aiming for social good.

Data intermediary An entity that can act in a range of ways to support the use of data, ranging from brokering between those generating data and those using that data, to more supportive roles curating, supporting and enabling collaborations between data providers and data users.

Data literacy Having the skills and competencies to work with data and critically reflect upon data practices, uses and possible risks.

Data mapping Data mapping is the process of matching fields from one database to another. It's the first step to facilitate data migration, data integration and other tasks in processes of working with data.

Data maturity A benchmark signifying that organisations have what is required in order to make optimal use of data.

Data sharing Where organisations share their internal datasets, subject to agreed consent, privacy and safety protocols.

Data sovereignty A way of understanding the importance of establishing consent and respecting the rights of, and ensuring benefits for, those who are the subjects of data.

Glossary

Data steward Organisational lead for data governance with responsibility for understanding the data that exists in organisations and ensuring data quality.

Data visualisation Data visualisation deals with the graphic representation of data. It is a particularly efficient way of communicating when the data is numerous as, for example, a time series.

Data walk A methodology to engage citizens with analysed and visualised datasets to help make decisions about their communities.

DataKind An international philanthropic franchise that harnesses the power of data scientists as volunteers, working with socially oriented organisations to explore potential from using data and to pilot data-driven innovations.

External data Data that can be accessed and used by a non-profit organisation that comes from sources other than the non-profit organisation itself.

Geospatial data visualisation A type of data visualisation that organises and presents data by location.

The GovLab A policy institute based at New York University that targets capability-building for public sector governance.

Internal data Data generated by a non-profit organisation through their work.

Meta-data Data that describes other data. Metadata adds descriptive information for items, like a case note or an image, provides information about structural features or administrative information, like permissions.

Named entity recognition A form of natural language processing (NLP) that seeks to find and classify named entities, such as proper nouns, people and organisations in unstructured text or documents.

National Neighborhood Indicators Partnership (NNIP) US-based data for social good learning network initiative with the goal of building data capability for communities to advance equity and well-being.

Natural language processing (NLP) A set of computational techniques for processing and analysing natural language, such as documents, social media posts or speech.

NESTA A UK-based social innovation think tank.

Non-profit organisation A social mission-oriented organisation or community group that does not operate to pursue profit or that reinvests profit to advance a social mission.

Open data Data that is freely available for use, either directly or conditionally open (subject to a risk assessment or research protocol).

Open Data Institute UK-based non-profit with a mission to raise the capability of people and organisations to work more actively with data.

PowerBI A data visualisation tool developed and published by Microsoft.

Glossary

Re-used data Data generated from non-profits' own operations which they analyse (or re-analyse) for insights.

Shapefile A geospatial vector data format for geographic information system software.

Topic modelling A type of statistical model for discovering the abstract 'topics' or clusters that occur in a collection of documents.

Unsupervised learning model Machine-learning algorithms that learn patterns from data without any 'training' or labelling by people.

Index

A
Artificial intelligence (AI), 106

C
Case study comparison, 30
Case study 1, 28, 38
   collaborating partners, 31
   datasets, 32–33
   findings, 36
   methods, 34
   origins, 31–32
   outcomes, 38
   project description, 29–31
   project goal, 29
Case study 3, 29, 58
   collaborating partners, 49
   data analysis, 52–53
   datasets, 51
   findings, 53–54
   methods, 51–52
   origins, 50
   outcomes, 57–58
   project description, 49
   project goal, 48
Case study 2, 28, 48
   before and after
      interviews, 46–47
   collaborating partners, 39–40
   data analysis, 43–44
   datasets, 41–42
   findings, 44–46
   methods, 42–43
   origins, 40
   outcomes, 47–48
   project description, 39
   project goal, 38
Center for Urban and Regional
   Affairs, 76
Citizen data literacy, 102

Citizen engagement, 17–18, 20
Collaborative data action, 2, 15
  learning by doing, 68
  process for non-profits data projects, 69
Collaborative data action methodology, 67–74
  finding data collaborators, 74–76
  steps, 70, 71
Community resilience dashboard, 1
Community services outcomes tree, 11
Consumer data rights laws, 102

D

Data
  benefits of collaboration, 91
  collaborators, 75, 95
  culture, 79
  data for social good, 2, 68
  data walks, 72
  ethics and consent, 79–83
  external, 3, 9–10
  good use of, 8–9
  harms, 13–20, 97
  initiatives, 113–118
  institutions, 98
  intermediaries, 75
  internal, 3, 9
  literacy, 14
  locational data, 11
  management, 64
  maturity, 14
  non-profit sector and, 4–7
  open data, 9
  outcome data, 9
  qualitative, 11
  quantitative, 11
  sensitive data, 80
  sharing, 100
  sovereignty, 18
  stewards, 78, 98
  temporal data, 11
  that non-profits might use, 9–10
Data analytics, 2, 8, 103
Data capability, 3, 13
  community model, 67
  field-building and, 91
  framework, 66
  future research, 106
  organisational competence and, 90–91
  philanthropic support of, 99
  three stages of non-profit's data capability, 93–94
  understanding, 64–67
Data co-op platform, 84, 98
Data governance, 65, 76–79
  ethics, protocols and policies, 81
  responsible data governance, 77
DataKind, 100, 116
The Data Lab, 118
DECODE Project, 102, 117

F

Five Safes model, 83
Framework for Measuring Data Maturity, 66

G

The GovLab, 114

I

Indigenous cultures, 4
Indigenous data sovereignty, 18

N

National Neighborhood Indicators Partnership (NNIP), 19, 72, 105, 115
NESTA, 114
New data perspective, 11–13
Non-profit data capability, 6
Non-profits, 5
   collaboration between, 7
   definition, 2
Non-profit sector, 4
   data and, 4–7
Non-profit starvation cycle, 6
Not-for-profit industrial complex, 5

O

The Open Data Institute, 115
   Data Ethics Canvas, 81

R

Re-use data perspective, 11–13

S

Social justice activism, 92

The manufacturer's authorised representative in the EU is Springer Nature Customer Service Centre GmbH, Europaplatz 3, 69115 Heidelberg, Germany. If you have any concerns regarding our products, please contact ProductSafety@springernature.com

Printed and bound by CPI Group (UK) Ltd, Croydon, CR0 4YY

25/03/2026

02078179-0009